EXPORTING PROSPERITY[tm]

Why the U.S. Economy may never recover...

James H. Boudreau

ISBN: 0989897303
ISBN-13: 978-0-9898973-0-3

Dedication

This book is dedicated to my parents and to my grandparents. Through their words, and more importantly through their actions and their character they taught me the importance of hard work, dedication, loyalty and integrity. Only heaven knows where I would be in this life without their example...and I wish the world had more people like them today.

Table of Contents

Introduction

Like many books, these pages are the culmination of a lot of "bottled energy", if you want to call it that. And as I sit at the keyboard I'm not sure if it is going to end up a long "rant", as comedian Dennis Miller would put it, or if it is going to end up a rational presentation of statistics and facts, opinions and ideas. But if you and I both make it to the last page we can each decide for ourselves. What I promise for us both is that these pages will be as candid, honest and true as I can make them, and without the censorship of political correctness. Like it or not, together we must all face a number of hard truths and make the choice if and how we will deal with them together and as individuals.

This story can begin almost anywhere…as a case of personal frustration with the current state of affairs, or as an expression of hope that there might be some daylight at the end of the tunnel. Like most Americans my life began with amazing aspirations, hopes and dreams, many of which I still hold dear. And while I have been very fortunate to have achieved many of those aspirations, there are many that I still hope to realize. Unfortunately, however, our dreams for the future are almost certainly going to come a lot harder than those of the past, that is if they come at all.

If you are reading this, it would be my hope that you retain some of my inherent optimism. I also hope that you share my acceptance of the harsh realities of our time coupled with a belief that we, as Americans, can accomplish virtually anything that we set our minds to. The question is can we do it by working together, as so many generations that have come before us? Or will "forces" continue to drive us apart as has been the case in recent years.

I will apologize in advance if you find the tone of my words to be overly-patriotic at times, but I do believe we live in the greatest country on Earth. And I believe that this greatness has come as a result of the passion, dedication and selflessness of so many that have come before us all. I also believe that honor and dedication are the qualities in mankind that will ultimately restore the prosperity that we have been so privileged to enjoy for so many generations.

Beyond my sense of patriotism, I hope you will also find in my words an equivalent sense of humor, if not sarcasm, as I believe in laughter as deeply as I believe in hard work and dedication. Besides, if we don't sometimes find a way to laugh at things the only alternative is to cry. Hopefully as we make it through these pages you will share the many emotions, high and low, that led to their creation. And if you find yourself asking more tough questions, of yourself, your neighbors, your company and/or your government, then all the "bottled energy" that went into these pages will not have been in vain.

And so we begin…

Chapter 1 - Why are we here?

It's only business, not personal…

There are few among us that haven't endured some level of frustration in the course of our professional lives, some of us more than others. Obviously I use the term "level of frustration" loosely as many people's experiences have been demoralizing, if not downright debilitating. Who doesn't know somebody that has had to re-start their career in their 40s or 50s through no choice of their own? And how many people do we know that have been unemployed for months, if not years, despite education, training, experience, etc.? How many people do we each know that want to work desperately but cannot find even the most basic of jobs?

If you are a business owner, or like me, a small business owner, how many people have you had to lay off temporarily or outright let go? How many times have you had to dig into the credit cards to keep things moving? How many investments would you like to make in equipment or facilities or people but cannot for lack of cash or credit? How many times have you been told by the bank "sorry, but it doesn't fit within our guidelines…"? Having spent a good portion of my career as a consultant as well as a small business owner I cannot count the times that I have personally witnessed these situations playing out.

How many times have you heard the expression "*It is only business, not personal…*"? For me personally that expression that makes me walk in circles shaking my head and fists seeing how many different shades of red my face can become. Why don't the people that use this expression be honest and just say what they truly mean, in more direct language?

> *"I am going to screw you over… I could probably find a way to avoid doing so if I tried, but since that would cost me instead of you I'm going to do it to you anyway…"*

If they did express it this way at least they would be honest with themselves and with you…because when someone takes away your livelihood and your ability to put food on the dinner table, it is VERY personal for you!

Figures Lie & Liars Figure…

The problem with statistics is that they consist of numbers… Because they consist of numbers we all assume that they must represent some truth. Numbers somehow seem "pure". We tend to trust them, especially when they are "official numbers", published by the government or some other "credible" source. But as has been said many times, "liars figure and figures lie"…not that we have any reason to be cynical… It does remind me of a story which I cannot confirm to be truth, rumor or urban legend…but it would be hard to believe that this scenario didn't play out in some CEO's office at some time and place:

> **XYZ Company, in the course of hiring a new Chief Financial Officer had narrowed down the list of candidates to a final 3. The last interview was with the CEO, who asked each the same simple question:**
>
> > **"How much is 2 + 2?"**
>
> **The first 2 candidates answered quickly and proudly:**
>
> > **"4, of course!"**
>
> **The last candidate stated, with equal conviction:**
>
> > **"What number would you like it to be?"**
>
> **Guess who got the job???**

Please don't take this as a dismissal of statistics and numerical analysis in general. Quite the contrary; it is necessary that we use numbers and statistics to measure many things in business and in life, or in a multi-trillion dollar national economy. The trick is NEVER to accept "the numbers" at face value…and NEVER to accept that "the numbers" are the ONLY numbers! We all owe it to ourselves to dig deeper, to understand SPECIFICALLY what a given set of numbers is designed to represent. And beyond the intended representation of a set of numbers, what numbers make up those numbers… Confused yet???

Let's take the "Rate of Unemployment / Unemployment Rate" in the U.S. at the present time. How many times have we all heard that "things are so much better here than in Europe…where "unemployment" is in "double-digits"? What is seldom pointed out, however, is that they are comparing "apples and oranges". The Europeans calculate their unemployment rate differently, and hence make any direct comparison unreasonable. When it came to trying to paint a more accurate picture of the state of the U.S. economy, this seemed like a good place to start. So I sought to define and calculate the "Real Unemployment Rate" in the U.S. Then the "Real" fun began.

The first mistake I made was to try and decipher the volumes of statistics published by the U.S. Dept. of Labor, the U.S. Bureau of Labor Statistics, the U.S. Census Bureau, etc… Since they are "the authorities", the agencies that publish the "official numbers" on this topic, I assumed it would be a fairly straightforward process to break down their statistics and access the "raw data"... The deeper I dug, however, the more confusing the process became. I didn't totally give up right away…but I did need to step away from it for a while.

Once I was able to get my eyes uncrossed I decided to take a different approach. I thought that it was simply a matter of clarifying the definition of the term "unemployment rate", as the government publishes it?

I started by looking up the definition of the word "**unemployed**", and found a lot of synonyms…"**jobless, idle, out of work**..." That made sense. Then came the word "**rate**", which also has a variety of definitions, but for these pages I chose the simplest - "**a ratio between two things**…". Theoretically, therefore, the statistic we all refer to was the "**unemployment rate**" should calculate the ratio (e.g. percentage) of people not working to people available to work…or perhaps just to those people able to work. But "nnooooooooo"…that isn't even remotely close to how the government calculates it.

What I ultimately discovered is that there are so many classifications of working people that make up those that are "**employed**" and those that are "**unemployed**" it would make your head spin. For example, if you are no longer looking for work, e.g. you have given up, or have exhausted your unemployment; the "official statistics" do not count you as "unemployed". Not sure about you, but if I had exhausted my unemployment benefits and was still not working despite all of my best efforts, I would have a hard time with the government not considering me "unemployed". Or how about a person who takes any job, at much lower pay, out of simple desperation, just to put food on the table?

You probably asking yourself "does this mean we are being lied to?". In the absolute sense of the word, no... The statistics that are reported are accurate representations...of something... The question is, representations of WHAT?

The other obvious question is "WHY would we be presented with misleading statistics?". The answer to that question is one of those cases where "the ends just might justify the means" (as hard as it is for me to say...it is!). The reality is that, if people knew the complete and real truth about some things it could easily cause a sense of panic and makes things much worse.

As much as I personally find politics nauseating, it is a necessary evil of the job – to be as honest as possible without causing people's worst fears to be realized. At the same time, we as citizens cannot afford to "bury our heads in the sand" either, lest it becomes necessary to change our national bird to the ostrich.

The "Official Labor Statistics"

I am sure many would agree that we are now seeing levels of "real" unemployment that we haven't seen since the great Depression (the time of this writing is the early fall of 2013). The "official statistics" have been listing unemployment in the 8 - 10% range since early 2009. But these do not include the "underemployed" or "farm jobs", those that have given up, etc. And given how many people that I know personally that have been unable to find work, the "official statistics" just didn't make sense to me. Hoping to make some sense of it...and even perhaps to find a way to put some people to work, I started to dig even deeper... I will apologize in advance for the dry nature of this section...but numbers can do that to you.

Since the makeup of the current unemployment number is the one that made the least sense to me, I decided to start there…to try and understand what that particular "number" really meant. So I hope you will indulge me as I walk through the exercise that I undertook. And I will try to "back into a number" that will perhaps tell us more than the simple, government-published "Unemployment Rate".

Many statisticians and researchers might disagree with this simplistic approach, but it typically is their job to create complex hypotheses and theorems to identify factors and variables at work…blah, blah, blah… I have an MBA and can do the same math. The truth of the matter is that, the more complex the equation, the more variables that it includes, the more easily it falls apart. So I decided to try and approach the "true unemployment number" via simple deductive reasoning.

Working Age Population – before we can determine "real unemployment", we need to know how many people are actually considered "able to work", as well as how many people live in the U.S. According to the U.S. Census Bureau (**www.census.gov**) there were approximately 315.1 million people living in the U.S. at the end of 2012, broken down into "working" age groups as follows:

	Population (millions)	Percent
Persons under 16 years of age	31.0	9.8%
Persons over 16	**243.3**	**77.2%**
Persons over 65	41.9	13.3%
Total	**315.1**	**100.0%**

Source – U.S. Census Bureau

For starters, I thought it was pretty reasonable to start with the **243.3 million** people that are "**of working age**", and work to deduce those who are working and those who are not…and for what reasons.

Employment Statistics – after reviewing the numbers from the U.S. Census Bureau, I moved on to the U.S. Bureau of Labor Statistics (**www.bls.gov**). I was encouraged initially to discover that their numbers were pretty close in terms of the total number of people of "working age", again roughly 243 million. From there my goal was to try and figure out how many people are actually working now, and ultimately compare that to historical data.

The first challenge was deciphering all of the different terminology in the various reports that I discovered, e.g. employed, unemployed, underemployed, etc. I was determined to keep it simple, so I started with the most commonly known statistic "unemployment", and in turn "employment". This is where it started to get "interesting".

U.S. Unemployment – Dec. 2013	Qty (millions)	Percent
Civilian Labor Force		
Employed	142.5	91.9%
Unemployed	12.5	8.1%
Total Labor Force	**155.0**	**100.0%**
Not in Labor Force	88.3	

Source – U.S. Bureau of Labor Statistics

I am sure you are right there with me with the question – "What do they mean by "**Not in Labor Force**"???". On one level I concluded that, at least in recent years, "Unemployment" has been calculated as a percentage of the "Labor Force". So, for at least a few years, we have been comparing "apples-to-apples". It is pretty easy to rationalize that unemployment of 6% a few years ago is "better" than 9.5% now. After all, 9.5% is not the same the 25% that we experienced during the Great Depression...or is it?

Different statistics were used to calculate unemployment during the Great Depression than are used today. There are many people that would argue that it has been as hard for them financially in recent years as they could ever have imagined, even in the Great Depression. I am not trying to provoke a debate on economic theory...just trying to figure out how many people are not working and why. And perhaps find out if there are more people that should be included in the "Labor Force" and "unemployment" numbers?

Not In Labor Force – This is where things really started to get more interesting, if not more confusing. Rather than drive myself nuts, again I

8

did everything I could to "keep it simple". From the same reports at the U.S. Bureau of Labor Statistics (**www.bls.gov**) I was able to pull out a few more numbers that made at least some sense regarding people that are working, or not. First, those in the 88.3 million that aren't counted in the "**Labor Force**":

Not in the Labor Force - 12/31/2012 (thousands)	
Do not want a job now (1)	**81,752**
Want a job (1)	**6,558**
Did not search for work in previous year	3,390
Searched for work in previous year, but not in past 4 weeks (2)	3,168
Not available to work now	651
Marginally attached (available to work now) (3)	2,516
Discouraged over job prospects (4)	909
Reasons other than Discouragement	1,608
Family Responsibilities	229
In School or Training	339
Ill health or Disability	168
Other (5)	871
Total Not in the Labor Force	**88,310**

Footnotes

(1) Includes some persons who are not asked if they want a job.

(2) Persons who had a job in the prior 12 months must have searched since the end of that job.

(3) Persons "marginally attached to the labor force" are those who want a job, have searched for work during the prior 12 months, and were available to take a job during the reference week, but had not looked for work in the past 4 weeks.

(4) Discouraged workers are persons marginally attached to the labor force who did not actively look for work in the prior 4 weeks for reasons such as thinks no work available, could not find work, lacks schooling or training, employer thinks too young or old, and other types of discrimination.

(5) Includes those who did not actively look for work in the prior 4 weeks for such reasons as child-care and transportation problems, as well as a small number for which reason for nonparticipation was not ascertained.

Not sure about you…but a few numbers jump out at me:

"Want to work" - 6.6 million – if someone wants to work, but isn't working, that sure sounds like "**unemployed**" to me???

"Do not want a job now" – 81.8 million – are you kidding me???

If we add just the people listed as "wanting to work" to those the U.S. Government lists as "unemployed", we get an **unemployment rate of 12.1%**... Now we are making some progress...but I am still appalled by this...

81.8 million do not want a job now???

Sure, some people are independently wealthy...others might be stay-at-home Moms...others disabled... We certainly cannot fault any of them for not wanting a job... But there are certainly not 81.8 million people in those categories.

At the very least, we should move the 6.6 million that want a job back into the "work force". By the way, you may want to "file away" that 6.6 million number for later pages.

I gave a lot of thought to diving deeper into the "not in the labor force" numbers. As I thought about it, however, I remembered my commitment to try and keep the numbers to a minimum, and to not over-complicate things. Besides, even this level of detail is a very good start as it gives us a more real picture of the number of people that are "unemployed"...

...including an argument that Real Unemployment is over 12%

So, on we go to the next set of numbers...

The "Official Economic Statistics"

There are an almost infinite number of ways that we can measure the "health of the economy". This is just another reason people's heads spin when they attempt to make sense of "the official statistics". There is the "stock market" that is touted in the media almost every minute of the working day, the GDP (**Gross Domestic Product**), the Real GDP, the Unemployment Rate (as we've already explored), etc., etc., etc. Again, the challenge is figuring out which numbers are meaningful, if not more representative of the standard of living of the average American.

For the purposes of this book, I decided to take some of the simplest numbers. More importantly I decided to take the "numbers" that I felt told a story…that actually told an ACCURATE story…over time… Even more importantly perhaps, I tried to find the "numbers" that illustrate what is happening to the "real working people" in this country, and maybe even why it is happening. And lastly, the "numbers" that, when changed, translate to improvements in the standard of living for the average American citizen.

I recognize that by choosing to highlight my own list of particular statistics, I risk being labeled a hypocrite…but I will accept that risk. I accept that risk because I took the time to go through countless tables and data points. I graphed them, compared them and correlated them to each other. At the end of the day I will stand by these numbers as telling the "real story" about the state of our economy. Hopefully anyone that disagrees will do the same level of research before raising their hand.

Per Capita GDP – the problem with using *simple GDP* is that it is a **total number** and it doesn't relate the economic growth of the entire country to that of the **individual citizen**. For example, if population grows 10% and the economy only grows 5% the "economic growth" per person actually **dropped**. The following table will illustrate that point in more detail:

Year	Population (millions)	Total GDP ($ billion)	Change in GDP	Per Capita GDP	Change in Per Capita GDP	Difference
1992	256.51	$8,280	3.4%	$32,279	2.0%	1.4%
1993	259.92	$8,516	2.9%	$32,765	1.5%	1.3%
1994	263.13	$8,863	4.1%	$33,683	2.8%	1.3%
1995	266.28	$9,086	2.5%	$34,122	1.3%	1.2%
1996	269.39	$9,426	3.7%	$34,989	2.5%	1.2%
1997	272.65	$9,846	4.5%	$36,112	3.2%	1.2%
1998	275.85	$10,275	4.4%	$37,247	3.1%	1.2%
1999	279.04	$10,771	4.8%	$38,599	3.6%	1.2%
2000	282.16	$11,216	4.1%	$39,752	3.0%	1.2%
2001	284.97	$11,338	1.1%	$39,785	0.1%	1.0%
2002	287.63	$11,543	1.8%	$40,132	0.9%	0.9%
2003	290.11	$11,836	2.5%	$40,800	1.7%	0.9%
2004	292.81	$12,247	3.5%	$41,825	2.5%	1.0%
2005	295.52	$12,623	3.1%	$42,715	2.1%	0.9%
2006	298.38	$12,959	2.7%	$43,430	1.7%	1.0%
2007	301.23	$13,206	1.9%	$43,842	0.9%	1.0%
2008	304.09	$13,162	-0.3%	$43,283	-1.3%	0.9%
2009	306.77	$12,758	-3.1%	$41,588	-3.9%	0.8%
2010	309.35	$13,063	2.4%	$42,227	1.5%	0.9%
2011	311.59	$13,299	1.8%	$42,681	1.1%	0.7%
2012	314.69	$13,593	2.2%	$43,196	1.2%	1.0%
Total Change - 1992 - 2012						
	58.18	$5,313	**64.2%**	$10,916	**33.8%**	30.4%

There are a lot of ways you can choose to interpret these numbers. Perhaps the easiest way to look at them is to treat the "overall GDP" as one person, and the "per capita GDP" average as another person. If you apply this perspective, the first person's overall income went up a total of **64.2%** over the past 20 years, while the second person's overall income went up just over half that amount – **33.8%**.

One quick note, this does NOT equate to personal income. It is simply a measure of what the U.S. economy "produces" in total and then divided by the total population.

Another way to think of this is to take the average income in 1992 for two different families' and grow them by the same percentages. Let's say for the sake of discussion that the total family income for these two families in 1992 was $50,000. Apply these growth rates and in 2012 the first family's income totals **$82,085**; the second family's income totals **$66,909**. By the way, during that 20 year period, the cost of living has grown at the same rate for both families. Easy to see why so many families seem to be struggling more and more every year. Is there a simpler way to state this? Sure…

The population is growing faster than the economy…consequently individual "prosperity" isn't growing at the same rate.

A professional economist might at this point accuse me of comparing "apples and oranges", as per capita GDP doesn't translate directly to individual personal income. To this criticism I would simply reply that, for an individual to earn a living, the dollars that fund that individual personal income must exist within the economy. GDP equates to what an economy produces, and in turn creates the trickle-down effect that eventually becomes personal income. Thus, if an economy produces less, e.g. earns less, then there are fewer dollars to spread among its populace.

The "Elephant in the Room"…the Trade Deficit

At the outset of this book I did promise to try and keep the numbers to a minimum…(ever notice that the first 4 letters of the word numbers is "**numb**"?). The problem is that, to understand the problem, and to possibly lay out some options for solutions, we do have to look at SOME of the numbers.

Statisticians have all sorts of tools at their disposal to sift through volumes of numbers to determine which statistics are meaningful. I won't profess to have done a complete and thorough analysis on every single available economic statistic. I don't know if one lifetime would be enough to do that level of analysis, nor do I think it would serve any useful purpose. I did, however spend hundreds of hours on the statistics included here, and I will say that some of them are so glaring that you cannot ignore them. In my opinion, the most glaring of all is the **U.S.**

Trade Deficit…the imbalance in the amount of goods and services purchased FROM the U.S. versus those purchased BY the U.S.:

Year	Imports	Exports	Difference	Diff. as a % of Exports
1992	$656,094,000,000	$616,882,000,000	-$39,212,000,000	-6.36%
1993	$713,174,000,000	$642,863,000,000	-$70,311,000,000	-10.94%
1994	$801,747,000,000	$703,254,000,000	-$98,493,000,000	-14.01%
1995	$890,771,000,000	$794,387,000,000	-$96,384,000,000	-12.13%
1996	$955,667,000,000	$851,602,000,000	-$104,065,000,000	-12.22%
1997	$1,042,726,000,000	$934,453,000,000	-$108,273,000,000	-11.59%
1998	$1,099,314,000,000	$933,174,000,000	-$166,140,000,000	-17.80%
1999	$1,230,764,000,000	$967,008,000,000	-$263,756,000,000	-27.28%
2000	$1,450,119,000,000	$1,072,782,000,000	-$377,337,000,000	-35.17%
2001	$1,370,065,000,000	$1,007,725,000,000	-$362,340,000,000	-35.96%
2002	$1,399,044,000,000	$980,879,000,000	-$418,165,000,000	-42.63%
2003	$1,514,482,000,000	$1,023,937,000,000	-$490,545,000,000	-47.91%
2004	$1,768,622,000,000	$1,163,724,000,000	-$604,898,000,000	-51.98%
2005	$1,996,171,000,000	$1,288,257,000,000	-$707,914,000,000	-54.95%
2006	$2,213,191,000,000	$1,460,792,000,000	-$752,399,000,000	-51.51%
2007	$2,351,925,000,000	$1,652,859,000,000	-$699,066,000,000	-42.29%
2008	$2,542,634,000,000	$1,840,332,000,000	-$702,302,000,000	-38.16%
2009	$1,961,844,000,000	$1,578,187,000,000	-$383,657,000,000	-24.31%
2010	$2,343,847,000,000	$1,844,468,000,000	-$499,379,000,000	-27.07%
2011	$2,669,663,000,000	$2,112,825,000,000	-$556,838,000,000	-26.36%
2012	$2,745,240,000,000	$2,210,585,000,000	-$534,655,000,000	-24.19%
Total	$33,717,104,000,000	$25,680,975,000,000	-$8,036,129,000,000	-31.29%

Source - U.S. Census Bureau, Foreign Trade Division

Just to be clear what this table illustrates… In the past 20 years, we have purchased more than **$8.0 TRILLION** (with a **T**, not a **B**) worth of goods and services from foreign countries, over and above what they have purchased from us!

To put this in perspective, let's put it in more individual terms. Let's say we have two very small villages, Smithtown and Jonestown. In Smithtown we have the heads of five households that earn and spend the family income – Al, Barbara, Charlie, Diane & Ed.

One day Al buys $100.00 in goods and services from Barbara. Barbara takes her $100.00 and buys $3.40 worth of "stuff" from people in Jonestown (who never purchase anything from anyone in Smithtown). Barbara takes her remaining $96.60 and uses it to buy goods and services from Charlie. Charlie takes his $96.60 and buys $3.28 worth of "stuff" from people in Jonestown, leaving him with $93.32. Charlie takes his remaining $93.32 and buys good and services from Diane...and so on and so on... You don't have to be a Nobel laureate to see what happens if that trend continues unabated.

Looking at these numbers from yet another perspective, take just the **$534.7 billion** trade deficit created in 2012, and apply the following logic:

- First, in the name of being conservative let's cut the number in half, since what we purchase is not all "labor"; much is "raw material". So, for the sake of discussion, we'll use **$262.3 billion** as our baseline.

- Again, for the purpose of this exercise, let's say that it costs an average company $50,000 per year for an average employee (assuming a reasonable American wage plus benefits, taxes, insurances, etc.).

- This translates to an annual salary for **5.3 million people**. (hmmm....how close is that number to the 6.6 million people that "want to work", but aren't considered by the government to be "unemployed").

- This only represents **1 year**!

Perhaps this is an over-simplistic illustration; however, few can argue with the logic or the pure numbers. We can just as easily work the formula backwards and ask the question, how much money does it take to create **5.0 million jobs**? **$250.0 billion** would certainly provide for a good start!

To see the real impact of this, let's track the "Deficit Ratio" (the trade deficit as a percentage of our overall exports) and compare that to the growth of the overall economy (GDP growth percentage) and the "unemployment rate":

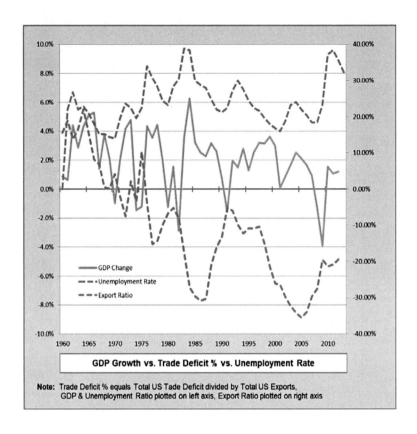

GDP Growth vs. Trade Deficit % vs. Unemployment Rate

Note: Trade Deficit % equals Total US Tade Deficit divided by Total US Exports,
GDP & Unemployment Ratio plotted on left axis, Export Ratio plotted on right axis

At first glance, the data doesn't seem to correlate; however, that is easy
to explain. Not everything happens at the same time, particularly when
you consider something as large as the U.S. economy. Whatever you
call it, "trickle-down effect", etc., one thing takes time to affect another in
an entity as large as a national economy. So, if we "slide" the lines to
add a "lag effect", here is what we get.

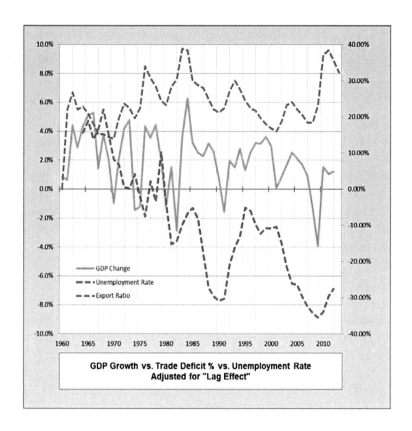

GDP Growth vs. Trade Deficit % vs. Unemployment Rate Adjusted for "Lag Effect"

What did I do? I simply "slid" the "Export Ratio" forward by four years, which shows what would happen if an increase in the trade deficit took effect immediately. Put another way, this would suggest that it takes four years for a change in the trade deficit to impact the unemployment rate and the economy as a whole. A few more key points to note:

- It takes approximately 1 year for a drop in the economy to increase unemployment.

- Our worst recessions since 1960 (1982, 1992, 2008) have followed a substantial drop in exports relative to imports in the preceding 4 years.

- When trade deficits increase to a point of being beyond 20% of exports, we are likely heading for a recession within four years.

- In the "modern economy" (post 1962) we didn't start to have such wild swings in our GDP and such extremes in our unemployment rate until after 1980, which is the same time when we started incurring larger and larger trade deficits.

The Snowball

In the 1980s we had a modest trade deficit, with a large portion of our imports coming with Japan. Japan has long maintained a protectionist trade policy, so a trade deficit with Japan was inevitable. Japan has a much smaller population than the U.S. however, so the harm to our economy from this deficit was a somewhat more limited that it is today, , not so inconsequential though.

The trade paradigm we began with Japan in the 1980s was, unfortunately, the beginning of a much larger "snowball effect" on our national "consumer psychology" and eventually our economy. We started to see an influx of less expensive products in a number of categories, particularly cars, consumer electronics and computers.

The first turn of the "snowball" came as numerous U.S. manufacturers started to go out of business, unable to compete with this new extreme price competition. The "snowball" started to gain size and momentum when it created an embedded "spending mindset". The TV, and before that the radio, used to be a place in the home where the entire family would gather to take in the "program of the night". There was ONE in each house and that was OK. Over time we got used to having 1, then 2, then 3 TVs, then VCRs, then DVD players, then audio systems, etc., etc., etc. Mass consumerism was born. Not to mention going from 1 to 2 cars in the driveway...or more if a household has teenagers with a license.

Over time our trade with Japan bolstered their economy, eventually to the point where the Japanese standard of living was fairly close to that of the U.S. This lifestyle came with a price...increased wages to Japanese workers, which lost Japan their lower labor cost advantage in international trade. They made a successful transition, however, to a focus on quality and innovation, and made investments in factories in the U.S., ultimately preserving much of the market position they hold to this day.

The void created in world markets for low-cost labor was quickly picked up by South Korea in the early 1990s and soon thereafter by China. With the way labor is calculated and subsidized in China, the labor content of most products was reduced to almost zero. They began to dominate numerous industries, one after another, forcing companies selling products in the U.S. to either go out of business or move their production overseas. Thus began and accelerated the demise of U.S. manufacturing.

Screw the Innovator…

It used to be that "dreamers" had a place in the U.S. economy, dreamers who could come up with a unique product or service and then capitalize on the opportunity they created for themselves. No more…

There are many components that make up our system of "intellectual property law" - patents, trademarks, copyrights, etc. Beyond the statutory law protecting these creative properties, there is another "common law" element known as "trade dress". In its simplest term, trade dress is a product design that is recognizable as being associated with a company or a brand, for example the look of a Gucci handbag, the shape of a Sharpie Marker, etc.

There was a time when trade dress was fairly easily protected…you simply needed to prove that you created a design for a product and that you used it in commerce in some capacity (i.e. you sold it). Wal-Mart, (along with many other large retailers) has made numerous, purposeful contributions to ending all that.

There was a point in time when Wal-Mart took great pride in purchasing and selling products made in the U.S.A.; something they touted quite loudly. That has since changed…dramatically. In many cases the price pressure that Wal-Mart started to put on their suppliers forced them to take their manufacturing overseas. Over time, with more and more companies taking their manufacturing overseas, there were less and less "made in the U.S.A." products for anyone to buy. This was the "beginning of the end".

Eventually Wal-Mart created an internal "sourcing team". This team would take designs presented to them by various manufacturers and entrepreneurs, bring them overseas (typically to China), and have a copy made under their own brand, or under a brand they created themselves. On the surface this would seem as illegal as it is unethical. A company called Samara Bros. Inc. thought so and sued Wal-Mart under the Lanham Act of the U.S. Constitution for violating their "trade dress".

The case of WAL-MART STORES INC. v. SAMARA BROS. INC. eventually made it all the way to the Supreme Court, and as hard as it is to believe, Wal-Mart prevailed. In March, 2000, the U.S. Supreme Court ruled that, for a product's trade dress to be protected, it must have "secondary meaning". Essentially this means that it must be recognizable in the market on some level. I can tell you from VERY personal experience that since this court case was ruled upon, "trade dress" protection has become harder to achieve, and close to impossible to protect.

This approach to product sourcing has been adopted by most major retail chains, which have set up their own internal "sourcing departments". These departments take the most successful products and the most promising designs and make "knock-offs" on a daily basis.

Next time you visit a major retailer take a look at the various product brands they offer and see how many you recognize. If it is a brand that is exclusive to that chain of stores, guess what... If it isn't a direct copy of a particular manufacturer's product, it is a lower cost alternative that required little or no product engineering or design by the retailer. They simply told an overseas manufacturer to "copy this, change that" so it is "just different enough".

You may be wondering how I can make these claims. First, I spent more than 18 years calling on many of the major retailers in the U.S., and have many friends that still do. I hear of their frustrations every day. I also have a particular situation that is playing out in the courts right now, where I have had to sue a major U.S. company for making an exact copy of a product I offer on one of my own web sites. Throughout the process they have been arrogant and belligerent, seeing their $5.0 billion size as justification enough for stealing my product design. I would tell you who they are but my attorney has prevailed upon me to wait until the court resolves the issue. Rest assured that once this case plays out the details will make it onto my various web sites…and quite possibly into its own book.

I don't know about you, but doesn't leave me particularly inspired to create new products and services, only to have other slimy individuals reap the rewards for my efforts.

Could it Be That Simple?

On the surface, YES, it is! If we are buying goods from other countries, we send them money. If they don't buy goods from us in return, that money is gone. To add insult to injury, they then loan us back that same money (plus interest), so we can buy even more of their goods.

So, if it is that simple, why isn't something being done about it? The U.S. government has spent TRILLIONS in so-called "stimulus" money over the course of the past 4-5 years. Why hasn't it made a difference in the availability of jobs to the average American?

1. Most of the jobs were temporary, e.g. highway projects (not that we don't need them…again a topic for later discussion) or other jobs that don't generate ongoing revenue.

2. A huge portion of the money that was given to these "projects" was spent on goods made overseas…contributing further to the trade deficit.

3. The money was borrowed to do it…but that is another discussion. Just think of it like using a credit card to buy your groceries…sooner or later you have to pay for them…with interest!

It would be easy to point fingers and lay out an infinite list of more examples of lunacy, stupidity, irresponsibility, etc., but that would only be me continuing to vent a lot of frustration. The more obvious question is:

"How did things get so bad and how do we change it???"…

Chapter 2 - We Lost Our Balance...

You are probably wondering what I mean when I say "we lost our balance"? For the purposes of this book I will say that the U.S. economy lost the balance between all of its "participants". To further clarify, "participants" includes individual workers, citizens, companies, the government, etc...anyone that receives or expends money in the U.S.

The Utopian View

In a "perfect world", all of the interests of all members of a group, in this case the U.S. economy, would be balanced. Everyone would contribute fairly and would receive their fair share of the proceeds of those contributions. This may sound over-simplistic, but we are talking about a "perfect world". So, let's start with a quick picture...imagine if you will a giant block of stone, balanced on a single point:

Since one of the focal points of this book is job creation, we'll examine a fictitious but typical company. In this case, as with most business, our "typical company" has four primary "stakeholders", stakeholders being those affected by the actions of a company. Imagine if you will, each of these stakeholders balancing on a corner of the block so delicately balanced above, each weighing the exact same amount.

In companies, as in life, everybody (i.e. every stakeholder) has their particular self-interest, and those self-interests tend to drive individual behavior. Things become problematic when one particular stakeholder is given more or less weight than the other. Eventually, the scramble begins...and everyone becomes "Humpty Dumpty".

As obvious as it may be, I feel it is still important that we examine the nature of each of these stakeholders to see if we can develop a deeper understanding. As many have said...sometimes we have to "walk in another person's shoes" before we can even begin to understand what drives them to behave in a certain way. So let's examine the each of the stakeholders from the standpoint of their individual "self-interest".

Employees – for the purposes of this book, we are going to consider anyone that is paid for work on some level to be an "employee". This can include self-employed, government workers, employees of large companies, small companies, etc. When it comes to employees, their "self-interest" can be simplistic or complex, but let's try to put it in basic economic terms to the degree possible:

- **Cash (i.e. Income)** – Nobody works for free, not for very long at least. Most people go to work to make the money they need to live and to accomplish their goals in life. And given that the cost of "things" almost never decreases, people will almost always have a need to make more money as time goes on.

- **Taxes** – While few want to pay taxes, it is a reality of being employed. When we make money, we create a requirement to pay taxes on taxes on our own behalf - federal, state, local, social security, etc. We also create an obligation for our employer, who must match a number of these taxes, and pay others, for example unemployment insurance. Every dollar that a company pays to an employee costs their employer an additional $0.15 - $0.35 (sometimes even more), depending upon location and other factors. At the end of the day, we have to earn the money that pays our taxes, the taxes that our government uses to pay its bills and to provide us with services.

- **Insurance** – Insurance is another reality in modern life...health insurance, life insurance, disability insurance, etc. There was a time that all of this insurance was a standard benefit provided to employees as part of their compensation. Unfortunately, this has become more and more costly in recent decades, not just in raw dollars, but as a percentage of wages. Depending upon the source you credit, most estimates for the cost of providing **just health insurance** for an average family can run from **$15,000 - $20,000** per year. That translates to $7.50 - $10.00 per hour that goes to the insurance company, whether paid by the employee or the company. Again, that is just health insurance...all of the other employee-related costs collectively add up to almost as much as that.

- **Job Security** – This is a long-lost concept in America, but that would take another entire book to explore. Even so, most people would prefer to have some security, or at least have some control over when they move on to another position.

- **Safety** – While some jobs are obviously more dangerous than others, it is reasonable to expect that employers will provide the safest possible working conditions for any profession. Safety is a more than reasonable expectation for anyone going to work, but it still costs money.

Customers – this is actually a very broad term that people relate to on many different levels. On one level, we are all "consumers", purchasing products and services every day. On another level, most companies that sell a product or service are also customers themselves for other products or services. This can be raw materials for a manufacturing company, utilities to power the lights in a store, etc. Regardless of whether you are an individual consumer or a corporate purchaser, it is likely that you expect most, if not all of the following:

- **Fair Prices** – It is hard to say when "price became everything" in American society. Consumers and corporate customers alike always think something can be less expensive. It could be a function of global competition, individual affordability or a conditioned response learned over time. Whatever it may be, we always assume we can find anything we want cheaper somewhere else, and will typically expend the effort to get it.

- **Selection** – George Carlin once said "Put two things together which have never been put together before, and some schmuck will buy it.". We all assume that, no matter what we want, somebody makes the thing we are looking for.

- **Availability** – Regardless of what we want, we also assume it is available immediately. This "sense of urgency" is largely an American quality, but we do expect whatever we buy to be delivered to us before we even knew we wanted to buy it.

- **Safety** – we expect things we buy not to injure or kill us. This may seem like another glaringly obvious statement to make, but it costs money to make products safer, so we need to mention it. And, by the way, it also costs money to provide the product liability insurance that is necessary to sell most products in most markets.

Suppliers – We, as customers, both personal and corporate, tend to assume that any company is lucky to have us…and we let them know that whenever they fail to acknowledge our importance! Personally, I am not one to settle for less than the highest quality product and service when I lay out my hard-earned cash. As a small businessman, however, I am on both sides of the equation and see both points of view.

- **Cash - Getting Paid** – Sometimes the biggest issue for a supplier, especially on the corporate side, is getting paid for your product or service. As a consumer, we pay for most things when we buy them, however companies are usually required to extend payment terms. Depending upon the industry, this can be very lengthy, sometimes many months. That means laying out the cash in advance to produce a product or service and not recovering that cash for, in some cases, almost a year.

- **Fair Prices** – Selling a product at a very low margin or worse yet, at a loss, benefits nobody in the end. A supplier that has their prices driven down has to find that money someplace. This usually results in laying off workers, sending jobs overseas, going out of business, etc.

- **Not Being Abused** – This might be considered a touchy topic, since most customers (individuals and companies) consider themselves to be "absolute royalty", reigning supreme over anyone to whom they bestow their business. Unfortunately, many companies and consumers, conditioned to getting whatever they want, take this to the level of abuse. Many major retailers have had to limit their return policies on TV's because of the number of people that buy them right before the Super Bowl and return them right after. This costs everyone else money as that TV has to be sold at a reduced price as "used". The retailer has to pay for that "discount" somehow, usually by marking something else up higher (ever look at the price of cables?).

Owners/Shareholders – The "Big Bad Wolf", demonized in the media almost daily, is "corporate greed". Evil companies, sending jobs overseas, screwing the American Worker, refusing to provide decent wages or health care, etc....bastards! It is easy to demonize some nebulous entity..."the company", "the government", "Wall Street", etc. After all, they aren't people anyway...right???

Now let's be real for a minute... We forget that the CEO of a massive company whose stock is traded on Wall Street is also a human being that goes to work to make money. In many regards he/she is no different than the owner of the local pizza shop...in that the money he/she makes typically comes not only from a salary but also from the profits made by the business.

Why would you start your own business? To make money! Why would you invest money (in a business, in the stock market, in a savings account, etc.)? To make money! On one hand we demonize Wall Street for their greed…yet if they aren't greedy enough our IRA doesn't grow fast enough. If companies don't make money their stocks don't increase in value and our personal investments don't grow. So, all that said, what do those "owners" want?

- **Return on Investment** – If we invest our time and/or money, whether as the owner of a small business or as a shareholder of a large company we want a return on our investment. That is why we invest!

- **Low Taxes** – Few would argue that the "government" is among the least efficient "business" entities in existence…whether local, state or federal. This is probably because nobody is pressuring them to make a profit. If they have money they spend it (and lately even if they don't have money they spend it). Any money that a company pays out in taxes is money that cannot be invested back into the company to make things better for everyone involved.

- **A Good Day's Work** – for a company to be profitable they need their employees to be productive. Unfortunately the expectation in recent times seems to be less hours for more pay, and that it is OK to spend half of the work day on Facebook, Twitter, Pinterest, YouTube, eBay, etc.

A Pile of Broken Eggs

While we all wish everyone could have everything they want, and that life would be fair to all, that is unfortunately not reality. We live and work in a global economy and with the U.S. population representing less than 5% of the world's population, our particular "rules" and "wishes" don't count for much.

It is a simple and glaring reality that we, as American workers and citizens, are part of the global economy and for the foreseeable future are going to have little choice but to live by its rules. At the very least, we will continue to be affected by them.

So what do we do? The first thing is to look in the mirror, as individuals, companies, special interest groups, citizens, workers, consumers, etc., and acknowledge how we got here. Not having lived in any country but the U.S. it is hard to say whether or not it is an "American thing", but we ARE experts at playing the **"blame game"**. And unfortunately the next few paragraphs will probably seem like I am doing the same thing…except perhaps that I am looking at everyone. The purpose of this is not to "throw stones", but to try and look at things from everyone's perspective. Perhaps more importantly it is to suggest where a little less selfishness on everyone's part might have led us to a different place than we are in now. Or, maybe even to help chart a path to a better place for us all.

Customers – Somehow we as a country have become a consumer economy. While it may be a painful realization, it equates to us being the world's locusts. Consume everything, produce nothing and sooner or later there is nothing left to consume. Think of it this way… Imagine if we all continued to eat the food that we eat every day…but our farms did not re-plant the crops, or if they only planted enough each year for 96.6% of the population… How long would it be before we all went hungry? Remember our example above with Al, Barbara, Charlie, Diane & Ed? Think this is a myth?

Over the past 20 years, our trade deficit has averaged 3.38% of our **total economy** per year. This means that out of every $100.00 we spend, $3.38 disappears. Getting back to the example above, an economy, like a society, is **cooperative** (or not…). When we go to work we earn money because someone is paying us for our time, e.g. the product or service we provide. We take that money and we give it to others, buying their products and services, and so on, and so on and so on… If, however, every year we "burn" some of that money by sending it out of the country, spending it on product NOT MADE IN THE USA, we reduce our neighbor's ability to buy the services WE MAKE OURSELVES. Let me say it again:

Every year that we spend money on goods NOT made
in the USA, we reduce our neighbor's ability to buy
the product or services that WE MAKE OURSELVES!

Next time you are out shopping, let's say for the 4th flat panel TV in your house, imagine the following scenario. You see two TVs standing next to each other, EXACTLY THE SAME IN EVERY WAY, except, one is made in Asia, the other in the USA… The TV made in Asia is priced at $600; the one made in the USA is $1,800. Which one do you buy???

No wonder TVs are no longer made in the USA (I did find one company assembling them here using overseas parts, but that was as close as I could come). What it comes down to is this…we all want lots of "stuff"…and every day we make our giant retailers rich selling it to us. If we all, as consumers, were willing to pay higher prices to buy American-made products, we would be helping keep ourselves employed, even if perhaps it meant we had less "stuff" as individuals.

Employees – This is probably the most sensitive topic anyone could ever broach as a writer, or even in a one-on-one discussion for that matter. I have numerous friends and relatives that are union employees, as well as corporate managers and business owners. The reason I am going to venture into this "mine field" is NOT to "throw stones" or say that organized labor is a bad thing. Quite the contrary, organized labor has done amazing things over the years to improve conditions for workers in the U.S. and the world. However, as with every "group" highlighted in this section, it is necessary to examine the "self-interest" that is contributing to our economic challenges.

Is it reasonable to demand a reasonable wage, working conditions, benefits for any and all people working in America? Of course! As the title of this chapter indicates however, we are talking about BALANCE here. So, what is balance? Balance certainly ISN'T companies making massive profits while making all of their product overseas. But it also ISN'T companies being driven out of business because they cannot employ enough workers to deliver their product and make a profit.

Let's do some quick math… Let's say a company employs 1,000 people making "Yummy Pies"…and the average employee makes $25,000 per year. If you include health insurance, benefits, taxes, etc., the cost per employee to the company is at least $40,000 per year. That adds up to at least $40.0 million per year in wages and employee-related expenses. Add the cost of raw materials, factory operations, etc. and you are probably looking at $80.0 million per year in total expenses. Now, how do we come up with that $80.0 million, just to break even?

Say a single "Yummy Pie" sells to the supermarket for $2.50...the company has to sell 32.0 million "Yummy Pies" every year just to pay the bills...before ANY PROFIT. I'll spare you the rest of the math, but that translates to every employee making 615 "Yummy Pies" every week. What if, at maximum capacity, the company can only make 500 "Yummy Pies" per week, per employee? This translates to only $65.0 million in income, resulting in a loss of $15.0 million for the company. It doesn't take long for the company to go out of business at this rate.

Think this is story is fiction? Think again... While the names and numbers above are different, a very similar scenario played out in 2012 when Hostess Brands Inc., maker of the ever-famous Twinkie went out of business. The company had been unprofitable for a number of years, and worked diligently to lower all of its costs, including labor. The representatives for the employee's unions refused to make wages and benefits concessions. The end result - the company went out of business and closed its doors. Instead of working together and compromising, with everyone perhaps 10% less, everyone ended up making 100% less.

Countless industries in the U.S. have never recovered from similar situations...textiles, steel...the list goes on and on. As I said at the outset of this section, this is NOT a condemnation of organized labor or of the "working man". It is about compromise...about finding the "win-win"...or in many cases not.

The airline industry has a few good examples of companies and employees finding that "win-win". Take Southwest Airlines...they make their employees owners. Everyone has a stake in the company doing well and everyone shares its success. The other major airlines have been consolidating for years trying to get back to profitability. Some airlines have received concessions from their unions in return for profit sharing and other incentives, and have returned to profitability. Others have not and have either been forced to merge into another airline or have closed down entirely.

Bottom line – FIND BALANCE…find a way to make it in the company's best interests to give more to employees. This is done by lowering costs, increasing productivity and profits…and there is nothing wrong with asking that those gains be shared. Nor is there anything wrong with employees working to make their company more successful. Just throw away the traditional "job descriptions" and "union rules" and work together.

Suppliers – Of the four key stakeholders balancing on our platform, suppliers probably have the least leverage. Employees can strike or go elsewhere. Purchasing staffs can typically buy from a competitor. Owners are typically clueless beyond the bottom line. So, what "stones can we throw" at suppliers if they are so powerless? There are plenty…they are not exempt by any measure… And they are in just as much of a position to contribute to their own success or demise.

Suppliers are typically companies in their own right, subject to all of the dynamics mentioned in this section. They have to deal with their own supply chains, overheads, etc., all part of their own drive to be competitive and profitable. Often times, however these competing agendas put them in a position where they are hurting the very customers they depend on for their survival. They reduce quality, increase prices, reduce investment in new products, technologies, etc. This just creates a downward spiral that makes it even harder to compete.

So, what is a supplier to do to help maintain "balance"? They need to consider the other stakeholders' needs when they walk into their customers. Deliver higher quality than competitors…make your customers look good to their customers. Make your product or service easier to handle, use, manage, etc. than your competitors, making it easier on your customers' employees. Invest in new products, services, technologies, etc. that improve your customers' bottom lines. Make them partners in your success.

Owners/Shareholders – As I said above, it is only natural, if not fair, that people that invest their time and/or money achieve a return on that

31

investment. Where this gets out of balance is when shareholders (including individual business owners) get greedy. They start skimping on quality, hurting their customers. They start overburdening their employees, damaging morale and eventually, productivity as employees "wear down". They start screwing suppliers who may choose to offer their newest technologies, products, etc. to the competition.

Companies are usually complex "animals", with different constituencies (departments, etc.) pursuing different agendas, many of which may be in opposition to each other. For the ownership of a company, public or private, to realize the benefits of their investments they need to understand what contributes to a company's productivity both internally and externally. But it takes long term view to make sure that your own drive for profit doesn't put you at cross purposes with the other stakeholders upon whom you depend. This means looking long and hard at how companies drive their profitability with or without the perspective of the other stakeholders.

Most companies, whether they sell a product or a service, have some need to also buy products and services. The responsibility for securing those products and services typically falls upon the members of the company's "supply chain" or "purchasing staff". Their contribution to the broader "profit agenda" typically involves negotiating with suppliers, which often means a continual drive for lower costs. Sometimes however, this becomes very single-minded and ignorant of suppliers' needs to be profitable in their own right. When this is taken to the extreme, it can become unprofitable to do business with you, and can force a supplier to walk away. What if that supplier that you just drove away has the next, greatest "widget", but will only sell it to your competitors?

Then we have the "human resources" staff…or those charged with overseeing the broader needs of the employees…and often with negotiating salary, benefits, etc. There are myriad problems with this conflict of interest. On one hand they are charged with making sure the employees are taken care of. On the other they are charged with negotiating to keep costs down. Getting costs down invariably means reducing benefits and/or salaries, either one-on-one or via union contracts. And when it comes to hiring, it means trying to get the most qualified employee for the lowest money.

This makes sense of course, but in reality it has a variety of unintended consequences. The most damaging of these consequences is often losing the most qualified employees...either during the hiring process or during staff reductions. Recruiters often won't present the most expensive candidates for even first-level consideration, depriving the company of potential innovation and creativity. And when it comes to staff reductions they always go after the most expensive employees first. In many cases the most expensive employees are the ones with the most experience. Getting rid of them can reduce a company's ability to solve problems, innovate and/or compete. Worse than all that, this mode of operations drives the best employees, both existing and potential, to your competitors.

There are countless other aspects of a company's operations that can be explored to identify even more "cross-purposes". The thing to remember as an owner or shareholder is that the profits you seek often result from the efforts and contributions of others...customers, employees and suppliers. So ask yourself, how do you balance everyone's interests??? And, perhaps even better yet, what is THEIR incentive to help YOU achieve greater profits???

Is Balance Attainable?

Who knows! Where the never-ending pursuit of self-interest begins and ends is probably a "question for the ages". Whether we like it or not, we Americans, all 315.1 million of us (and counting), are in this together. And if we want things to improve in this country we are going to have to work together. The solution requires compromise and at least some degree of selflessness. It requires adversaries to get on the same side of the table and become partners against the "problem", which is the real enemy, and not against each other. Ultimately this means learning to "walk in another man's shoes"...maybe something to the effect of the following:

Employees – Whether you are negotiating via a union, voting through your union or negotiating on your own behalf, be aware of your company's situation. Are they profitable? Are they growing? Most of us don't have the luxury of picking and choosing who we go to work for as jobs are hard to come by these days. We can, however find balance with the company we do work for. We can forego some salary in favor or profit sharing. We can negotiate incentives for productivity gains. There are a lot of ways that we can make it easier for a company to compensate us better. But we have to be willing to "give" if we expect to "get".

Consumers – Look at the labels and be conscious of what you are buying, particularly where it is made. I am sure that the more you do this the more you will become horrified at how few products are actually made within our own borders any more. And the term "Made in the USA" can be misleading…"Made in the USA", "Manufactured in the USA" and "Assembled in the USA" each mean a different level of "U.S. content". And to make it even more complicated, those labeling requirements can vary according to the state you live in.

To buy products where some aspect of its manufacturing has been completed in the U.S.A. may mean spending more money. And it may mean taking more time to find and shop with specialty retailers, on street and online, who deal with the smaller suppliers that don't use a container ship to bring in all their merchandise.

Suppliers – I said above, suppliers, being companies themselves, have their own agendas related to profitability, etc. In this single capacity, as a supplier to their customers, they can be a key ingredient in that customer's success. A supplier can choose to view the customer as an enemy, holding back the best price, the latest product offerings, insights about future developments in the industry, etc. Or, they can make the customer a partner, give them incentives to draw business away from competitors, provide insights that improve their competitive position, etc.

Owners/Shareholders – If selfishness has any proportion in this equation, most would point the finger at the owners and shareholders of a company first. In reality, it IS their money, to invest and spend how they choose, however foolishly or insightfully, however selfishly or altruistically.

Unfortunately, many investors, at least the type that we typically see in the public stock markets, tend to be short-sighted. They will sacrifice long-term profits in favor of immediate "bumps" in a stock price. A case can be made, however that, long-term growth is not that far in the future when it is consistent growth. This comes from "sharing the wealth" with employees...whether it be stock options, profit sharing, etc... Make it worthwhile for employees to contribute to the "corporate agenda". Invest in equipment and facilities that make it easier to deliver higher quality and productivity.

The result will be a company with higher morale, capability and creativity, all of which contribute to growth and profitability. In short, make the other 3 stakeholders partners in your success and you will ultimately serve your own interests better.

Chapter 3 – Where is the Government in All This?

As I begin this chapter, the first thought that comes to mind is "how do I control my emotions and frustrations as I write it?". But then again, should I even try???

The U.S. Federal Government alone is spending $3.7 TRILLION in 2013...which is $1.2 TRILLION more than they are taking in. This grew the U.S. National Debt to $16.7 TRILLION. Sorry to keep capitalizing TRILLION, but it is just staggering to me. This translates to $53,870 owed by every man, woman and child in the U.S. This isn't personal debt in the traditional sense, however it is money that OUR government spent that WE will have to pay back someday...somehow... Just in case you were wondering how the national debt gets paid back??? In the same way the government gets the other money it spends...taxes!

But then again, the politicians can just "kick that can down the road" and leave it for the next guy in office to take care of...or for your grandchildren and their grandchildren to take care of. They've been doing it to us for years and we keep letting them...and then we keep re-electing them.

Imagine if your household took in a total income of $50,000, but your family went out and spent $74,000. BUT, you didn't have that $24,000 in savings, so you borrowed it...on top of the $310,000 that you are already in debt. Oh, by the way, out of your annual budget, you are paying roughly $7,200 in interest. Guess what? That IS how the proportions would translate for a household with a family income of $50,000. And, at the risk of repeating myself, the Federal Government has created a debt of $53,870 (and counting) that every individual in this country, who will have to pay back eventually via some form of taxation.

You may be asking why I am diving into the Federal Budget and National Debt now, when I've already concluded that the Trade Deficit is the primary culprit in our economic woes??? First, the government's ineptitude is largely at fault for many aspects of our economy getting into this state. And second, it is just so infuriating!!!

I am not "talking out of both sides of my mouth" by here pointing the finger at a "nebulous entity". I will, in the pages that follow, drill down to a few specific departments and policies as examples of where the government is part of the problem and not part of the solution…

Irreversible Force Meets Immovable Object…

The sub-title of this book is "Why the U.S. Economy May Never Recover"…which is a fairly bold statement. The reason I believe this to be so is because I cannot see our political process ever reforming itself. And, as long as our political process remains unchanged, so will continue the government's inability to solve problems.

Our elected officials are not put in place because they are skilled at dealing with the real problems of society or the economy. They are put in place because they are good politicians, essentially because they are good at telling people "what they want to hear". Give people bad news, i.e. the truth, and they won't vote for you.

The other major problem is that voters don't put people in office…money does. Unless a candidate can stay in front of the people long enough, often enough to convince them of their particular "message", they will never get elected. That costs money, and that money has to come from somewhere.

What is most infuriating to me as an individual voter is how many election campaigns are funded largely, if not primarily by money from special interests. You may find this incredible, but think about it. We hear about election corruption in other countries all the time, but we assume our elections are "clean as a whistle". In truth, if our system was incorruptible, there would be no means whatsoever of special interests financing election campaigns.

As an individual voter we cannot make contributions totaling more than $2,600 to a particular candidate (*2013/2014 Federal Election Commission Limits*). A Political Action Committee (PAC) however can give any amount of money to any candidate. So, if a special interest, an industry, company, etc., wants to "buy" influence in Washington, all they have to do is pump a ton of money through a PAC to a candidate who favors their point of view. That money in turn creates candidate greater exposure for the chosen candidate, usually followed by a victory…and the puppet strings are in place.

Why would any politician ever change the system that gets them elected??? They won't...it is not in their "self-interest"; so we will continue to get "professional politicians" in office...and not dedicated, skilled "servants of the people" as envisioned by the Founding Fathers.

Unfortunately the election of "special interest puppets" is only the first level of inequity that befalls the average citizen each election season. Immediately after these pols are swept into office, they make their staff appointments. Depending upon the office, there might be party positions, cabinet positions, department leadership positions, etc. And into those positions are placed people that are owed favors, not those most qualified to do the job. And we wonder why we see scandal after scandal, misstep after misstep by our various politicians and government agencies.

As obvious as it may seem, I will state it anyway – actual job experience and credentials are the last thing considered when someone is appointed to a very senior leadership position in government. And with inept leadership we expect the staff to be better???

The "Federal Department of Economic Squander & Impairment"

After 9/11 the government merged a number of different departments to form the Department of Homeland Security. These various departments had common purposes that were pretty obvious – chief among them keeping the American people safe – making it sensible to unite their forces.

In that same spirit, there are a number of other departments that I feel should be united as they appear to have very common goals. It would be unrealistic to suggest the total dissolution of these departments, so I am suggesting a merger, under a common series of objectives. The big challenge, as with any overarching new venture is the creation of a concise mission statement...but here goes...

"To spend untold billions of taxpayer dollars, while inhibiting creativity and eliminating opportunities for innovation and economic growth wherever possible"

OK, the sarcasm may be a bit "over the top", but having experienced first-hand the ineffectiveness, ineptness and total waste of space of these departments, I chose to exercise my 1st Amendment rights...;-). That does not, however, minimize the issues with these particularly useless bureaucracies. At least we can consolidate them and name them according to their evident purpose – again, the **Federal Department of Economic Squander & Impairment**. We can even use the ostrich or maybe the dodo bird in their official seal. And their motto can be "E Pluribus Destructum"... I may be on to something...

The Small Business Administration – Of all the departments of the Federal government that do absolutely nothing but waste money and space, the SBA may be the most shining example. As a small business owner and entrepreneur myself, I would expect the SBA to be my "best friend in government". Unfortunately I learned many years ago that they are nothing but a useless bureaucracy that benefits nobody save those it keeps on its own government payroll.

Some may consider these statements to be a bit harsh, but you have to consider the perspective. As a small business owner, I would expect a number of things from the SBA, in part based upon anecdotes passed on to me as a young manager in the 1980s. These expectations included among other things, grants to start or grow a business or loans for the same, and perhaps some advice on the mechanics of starting or running a small business. What I eventually discovered is that they offer NONE of the above. Having attempted to work with them several times in the 90's, here is what I discovered and which is still the case today:

- The SBA does NOT actually LOAN money...they simply provide a guarantee to a private bank who provides the actual loan. If you default on the loan, the government pays a portion of it back to the bank. The problem here is that, in most, if not all cases the SBA guarantee is harder to get than it would be to get the loan on your own. And, with or without the SBA guarantee, you still have to provide personal guarantees and collateral, typically your house. If you are going through that much grief you might as well just get a second mortgage in the first place.

- The SBA does NOT actually GRANT money. They may point you to another department of government that grants money for a specific purpose, that purpose NOT being to start or grow a business. But if you want to find out what kind of flies the North American Bullfrog prefers I am sure there is some government agency that will give you a grant to research it.

- The SBA does NOT even provide ACTUAL ADVICE. They have aligned themselves somewhat with a private organization called SCORE (Service Corps of Retired Executives). SCORE consists of thousands of independent volunteers who help counsel small business owners. This assistance is not funded by nor guided by the SBA. If the SBA disappeared, I doubt SCORE would be affected...they may not even notice.

The SBA Budget for 2012 was $918 million with a requested $1.1 billion for 2013. This may not seem like a big dollar amount compared to the overall Federal Budget, or the economy as a whole. But then again, that is how the government wastes so much money...a million here, a million there...a billion here, a billion there...

To put it in another perspective...take their $1.1 billion and give $1.0 million to 1,100 businesses to buy equipment and pay employees for some new product or venture. At 5-10 jobs per company that adds a decent amount of jobs versus the ZERO the SBA adds directly. They take credit for loans given in their reports, but those loans would be given without the SBA, since the business owners have collateralized the notes themselves.

The United States Patent & Trademark Office (USPTO) – I personally believe the heart of the U.S. economy is the creativity of the individual. As long as there has been a United States of America, there has been a spirit of innovation and invention...and this spirit has driven economic growth. This was recognized by the Founding Fathers who sought to protect this creativity in the U.S. Constitution (*Article 1, Section 8*):

"The Congress shall have Power ... To promote the Progress of Science and useful Arts, by securing for limited Times to Authors and Inventors the exclusive Right to their respective Writings and Discoveries"

This led to the formation of the United States Patent & Trademark Office, which issued its first patent in 1790. Since that time, the USPTO has issued almost 9 million patents and has administered the legislation protecting these patents as well as countless copyrights, trademarks and other intellectual property.

Unfortunately, however, this system of protecting intellectual property for U.S. innovators is largely "broken". I'll characterize "broken" on a few different levels, where the protections afforded under the USPTO are either ineffectual or valueless in all practicality. My commentary will of course be qualified.

- **Patents** – The protections afforded by a patent have always been intended to protect an inventor of some useful device, substance, process, etc., to allow that inventor to capitalize on their innovation. Over time, however, the patent system has become overburdened, if not corrupted under its own weight.

  First, with 9.0 million patents issued over 220+ years, it is hard to innovate in a way that is original and that doesn't violate another existing patent. Consequently, the Patent Office has become overly cautious, the result of which is that so many of the patents that are actually issued are so specific and narrow that they are easily circumvented by a competitor. Competitive advantage is, after all, the reason for obtaining a patent in the first place. In many cases a patent actually gives a competitor all the insight they need to work around your patent, if not usurp your innovation entirely.

  This is made even worse since the USPTO started publishing patent applications when they are filed, as opposed to when they are issued, giving competitors even more time and information to respond.

  Timing is yet another major issue...as it can take several years to obtain a patent. In many industries, by the time you obtain your patent, the innovation has been superseded by another.

- **Trademarks** – It really isn't necessary to delve too deeply into trademark law, as this part of the USPTO is, from my perspective working fine, even if its value is somewhat limited. The key value here comes when a trademark is "registered", whereby it is acknowledged by the UPSTO to be unique and distinctive. It is generally accepted however, that a trademark is considered protectable the instant it is used in commerce, even if it isn't registered, as long as it is unique and distinctive and doesn't cause any confusion in the marketplace.

- **Copyrights** – Like trademarks, copyrights are generally considered protected the instant a unique work is produced. The key difference here is that it extends beyond a word/name/brand, phrase or image, i.e. a trademark, in order to protect larger "works of art" (e.g. example movies, music, books, etc.) The challenge here is that the creator must largely police the protection of their properties themselves. With millions of "works" created over centuries, it is virtually impossible for any government entity, even with technology, to compare everything in existence to determine what might or might not infringe.

  The bigger issue with copyrights is a combination of culture and enforceability. In many countries intellectual property is considered "property of society", something everyone is entitled to share. This makes software, movies, music, etc. virtually impossible to protect in many countries. Even in the U.S., with the advent of music sharing services, it has become a cultural norm among younger generations to share music. Perhaps more importantly, it has created a mindset of "why pay for it when I can get it for free". When music and movies are among the most lucrative industries in the U.S., this mindset is perilous, as we are stealing from our own.

- **Enforceability & Practicality** – Overall, the issue is not whether or not you can obtain or maintain "legal" protection of your intellectual property. Ask any attorney that specializes in patents and/or other intellectual property and they will tell you "your patent is only worth something if you have the money to defend it". There are numerous cases where companies infringed upon the intellectual property of a company or an individual that did not have the finances to defend it…and ended up losing out on the profits of an invention that was LEGALLY PROTECTED.

Worse yet, often times, and as egregious as it is, some companies infringe other companies intellectual property knowingly and willfully. They simply make a calculated decision whether or not the company that owns the intellectual property has the finances to defend it. And that generally means $100,000 to start.

Unlike the SBA, I am not advocating the dissolution of the USPTO. This is one VERY rare instance where I would suggest expansion of a government agency. The USPTO needs to be **overhauled**, maybe even privatized. Some other key suggestions:

- **Confidentiality** – Keep patents confidential until published.

- **Timing** – Get enough examiners in house to evaluate and issue patents quickly, while they have value (and, set hiring standards that require examiners to have real-world experience in the category of invention they oversee). Perhaps even expand protections for patents when filed.

- **Cost** – Make it more practical to patent an innovation, particularly for those that may not be able to afford the roughly $20,000 that is necessary to cover attorneys and other costs. This would be a particularly good use of a "government grant program".

- **Enforcement** – Make it a criminal offense to violate intellectual property, as well as a civil offense. When executives start paying for IP theft with jail time as well as the royalties they should have paid in the first place, things will change. And, make available a defense fund to give qualified small businesses, inventors, artists, etc. the resources to defend their creations.

The United States Department of Commerce – OK, here is another major "waste of space"…although I have to admit that I have a harder time providing specific justification. Maybe that is the best justification…that I cannot figure out what they do? For starters, they DO spend roughly $3.0 billion a year.

Beyond the space they take up, the D.O.C, does provide a lot of really thick reports. By all accounts, however, the reports they publish are redundant, with all the same data available via the Bureau of Labor Statistics, the Census Bureau, the G.A.O. (Government Accounting Office), etc. Actually, maybe that's an even better idea...wipe out every department that does nothing but publish reports and merge them into one?   Wait...less cost to the taxpayers...consistent numbers...integrated reporting...that makes far too much sense... Sorry, what was I thinking???

The United States Department of Energy – Even mentioning the D.O.E. opens up another "can of worms", because of all of the complexities of our society (not to mention all the special interests tied to the petroleum industry). But, since this chapter is entitled "Where is the U.S. Government in all this?", and since energy is one of the most important drivers of our economy it cannot be ignored.

The D.O.E. was created in 1977, at the height of our first major "energy crisis", with the primary purpose of **reducing our dependence on foreign sources of oil**. What is laughable if not depressing, is that our energy imports as a percentage of our total usage **INCREASED**...from roughly 37% in the 1970's to more than 64% in the 2000's...(*U.S. Census Bureau – 938 – Crude Oil and Refined Products – Summary, 1973-2010*). What I find even more excruciating as an individual energy user and tax payer, is that, in virtually every year of the D.O.E.'s existence the cost of oil has increased and our dependence on foreign oil has increased.

The more I dug into "energy" in general the more I realized that really diving into this topic would require yet another book (if not a lot of aspirin...). There are, however a number of important statistics that come to bear as they relate to actions, if not inactions by our government.

For starters, let's look at the sources of our electricity (ultimately our most important energy resource) in the U.S. in 2010.

Electricity Generation Source - 2010	Billion Kw/Hours	% Total
Fossil Fuels		
Coal	1,850.8	44.9%
Petroleum	36.9	0.9%
Natural gas	981.8	23.8%
Other gases	11.2	0.3%
Total Fossil Fuels	**2,880.7**	**69.9%**
Renewable Energy		
Conventional Hydroelectric Power	253.0	6.1%
Biomass - Wood	38.0	0.9%
Biomass - Waste	18.6	0.5%
Geothermal	15.7	0.4%
Solar	1.3	0.0%
Wind	94.6	2.3%
Total Renewable Energy	**421.1**	**10.2%**
Nuclear electric power	807.0	19.6%
Other	11.2	0.3%
Total Electrical Generation	**4,120.0**	**100.0%**

Source: U.S. Census Bureau – 945 – Electricity Net Generation by Sector and Fuel Type

To put this in perspective, a kilowatt hour is 1,000 watts of electricity used for one hour. For example, 10 light fixtures with 100 watt bulbs used for one hour would result in 1 kilowatt hour of usage. So, our national use of electricity amounts to keeping approximately 41.2 billion 100 watt light bulbs turned on 24/7. And we use some kind of fuel to generate approximately 90% of that power. And fuel costs money.

Today the solar power industry estimates the "cost per watt" for the panels and infrastructure necessary to convert sunlight into electricity to be around $5.00 per watt. By the year 2017 this cost is forecast to have been reduced to under $1.00, perhaps even under $0.50 per watt. Unlike conventional sources, a solar panel isn't rated by "watt-hour", because it is a one-time cost. After the initial cost of the panels and infrastructure the actual electricity is virtually free, because the sun is free. There will be other costs associated with maintenance of the infrastructure, but that is a separate issue, and is still likely to be far less than the cost of maintaining the current grid and power plant system.

Imagine if we took $500.0 billion and invested it in giant solar farms in the middle of the various uninhabited desert lands across the U.S. That would generate 100.0 billion watts of electricity, or 2.5% of our current usage. If the price per watt continues to drop as forecast, say to $1.00 per watt, that same investment would supply 12.5% of our entire national usage of electricity, virtually for FREE!

Some of you are might be saying "wait a minute, the D.O.E. lost more than $500.0 million in the Solyndra "debacle". That is an example of the lunacy if not ineptness of government when it comes to specific implementations of innovation. The D.O.E. backed a specific company with a specific technology, essentially "betting the farm" on an unproven technology. In the end, changes in the competitive landscape for solar panels made other technologies affordable and made Solyndra irrelevant as a company. Instead, the D.O.E. could have simply given grants to the existing power providers to build renewable energy plants. Power companies are typically profit-making entities, so they have much greater incentive to build out the most effective solution.

In case you were wondering, the "American Recovery and Reinvestment Act of 2009" allocated only $16.8 billion out of more than $800.0 billion to "Energy Efficiency and Renewable Energy", a veritable pittance…

NAFTA – The *North American Free Trade Act* was intended to develop North America as a more significant economic force in the world economy by simplifying and encouraging trade within the U.S., Canada and Mexico. The problem again here is that, when you have a country with different labor rates and commercial regulation, the U.S. is put at an unfair disadvantage. Take a look at the following two tables examining our trade relationships with Canada and Mexico since NAFTA took effect on January 1, 1994:

U.S. Trade with Canada 1985-2012 (dollars)

Year	Exports	Imports	Balance	Deficit %
2012	292,539,700	323,936,500	(31,396,800)	-10.7%
2011	281,291,500	315,366,500	(34,075,000)	-12.1%
2010	249,256,500	277,636,700	(28,380,200)	-11.4%
2009	204,658,000	226,248,400	(21,590,400)	-10.5%
2008	261,149,800	339,491,400	(78,341,600)	-30.0%
2007	248,888,100	317,056,800	(68,168,700)	-27.4%
2006	230,656,000	302,437,900	(71,781,900)	-31.1%
2005	211,898,700	290,384,300	(78,485,600)	-37.0%
2004	189,879,900	256,359,800	(66,479,900)	-35.0%
2003	169,923,700	221,594,700	(51,671,000)	-30.4%
2002	160,922,700	209,087,700	(48,165,000)	-29.9%
2001	163,424,100	216,267,900	(52,843,800)	-32.3%
2000	178,940,900	230,838,300	(51,897,400)	-29.0%
1999	166,600,000	198,711,100	(32,111,100)	-19.3%
1998	156,603,500	173,256,000	(16,652,500)	-10.6%
1997	151,766,700	167,234,100	(15,467,400)	-10.2%
1996	134,210,200	155,892,600	(21,682,400)	-16.2%
1995	127,226,000	144,369,900	(17,143,900)	-13.5%
1994	114,438,600	128,405,900	(13,967,300)	-12.2%
1993	100,444,200	111,216,400	(10,772,200)	-10.7%
1992	90,594,300	98,629,800	(8,035,500)	-8.9%
1991	85,149,800	91,063,900	(5,914,100)	-6.9%
1990	83,673,800	91,380,100	(7,706,300)	-9.2%
1989	78,808,900	87,953,000	(9,144,100)	-11.6%
1988	71,622,000	81,398,000	(9,776,000)	-13.6%
1987	59,814,300	71,084,900	(11,270,600)	-18.8%
1986	45,332,500	68,252,700	(22,920,200)	-50.6%
1985	47,251,000	69,006,400	(21,755,400)	-46.0%

Source: U.S. Census Bureau

47

U.S. Trade with Mexico 1985-2012 (dollars)

Year	Exports	Imports	Balance	Deficit %
2012	215,931,200	277,569,800	(61,638,600)	-28.5%
2011	198,068,600	262,873,900	(64,805,300)	-32.7%
2010	163,664,600	229,985,600	(66,321,000)	-40.5%
2009	128,892,100	176,654,400	(47,762,300)	-37.1%
2008	151,220,100	215,941,600	(64,721,500)	-42.8%
2007	135,918,100	210,714,000	(74,795,900)	-55.0%
2006	133,721,700	198,253,200	(64,531,500)	-48.3%
2005	120,247,600	170,108,600	(49,861,000)	-41.5%
2004	110,731,300	155,901,500	(45,170,200)	-40.8%
2003	97,411,800	138,060,000	(40,648,200)	-41.7%
2002	97,470,100	134,616,000	(37,145,900)	-38.1%
2001	101,296,500	131,337,900	(30,041,400)	-29.7%
2000	111,349,000	135,926,300	(24,577,300)	-22.1%
1999	86,908,900	109,720,500	(22,811,600)	-26.2%
1998	78,772,600	94,629,000	(15,856,400)	-20.1%
1997	71,388,500	85,937,600	(14,549,100)	-20.4%
1996	56,791,600	74,297,200	(17,505,600)	-30.8%
1995	46,292,100	62,100,400	(15,808,300)	-34.1%
1994	50,843,500	49,493,700	1,349,800	2.7%
1993	41,580,800	39,917,500	1,663,300	4.0%
1992	40,592,300	35,211,100	5,381,200	13.3%
1991	33,277,200	31,129,600	2,147,600	6.5%
1990	28,279,000	30,156,800	(1,877,800)	-6.6%
1989	24,982,000	27,162,100	(2,180,100)	-8.7%
1988	20,628,500	23,259,800	(2,631,300)	-12.8%
1987	14,582,300	20,270,800	(5,688,500)	-39.0%
1986	12,391,700	17,301,700	(4,910,000)	-39.6%
1985	13,634,700	19,131,700	(5,497,000)	-40.3%

Source: U.S. Census Bureau

48

There are a lot of interpretations that can be made from this data, but the simplest and most obvious is that we had a more balanced trade relationship with our northern and southern neighbors before NAFTA than after.

Why? Some answers are easy... Mexico has lower labor cost than the U.S., as does Canada, although there isn't nearly the differential north of the border as there is south. One point to note is that, during our recessions of the early 1990s and late 2000s, our trade imbalance with Canada shrank. Much of what we import from Canada is lumber and building materials. If our economy is suffering, we aren't building and hence don't import as much from Canada. Regardless of the other factors at work in our overall economy however, Canada has benefited from NAFTA at our expense.

Government Waste in General

It would take a lifetime to document the billions of dollars wasted each year on an infinite variety of government inefficiency and waste. It actually makes me ashamed that I even hesitate to mention some of them because I might "offend someone". Maybe that is the biggest problem we face as a country – we are afraid to discuss "doing the right thing" because we might offend some individual. So much for the "greater good"...

Wherever you live, take one day, and pay extra attention to every interaction you have with anything funded and/or operated by the government, in whole or in part, and think about the waste. Want to drive yourself even more nuts? Take out a piece of paper or set up a spreadsheet and calculate the costs. Then extrapolate that over a year for a state, for a country, etc. Most experienced business people will tell you that they could deliver greater benefit to the people than the government does now, and do it for 20-25% less (if not more).

In Massachusetts, for example, all road construction projects use State Police "details" as "safety agents". They sit in their cars, burning fuel with their lights flashing. The object of this is noble and sensible...to make sure that people cannot possibly ignore the construction zone and that they slow down in order to preserve the safety of the workers, etc. It would be ludicrous to suggest that actions taken to ensure public safety aren't of critical importance. What is also ludicrous is the money we waste while doing it. We could easily deploy trailers that put on a world-class light show, powered by solar panels and accomplish the same thing at small fraction of the cost. The cost of a State Trooper in Massachusetts for these "details" – at least $40.00 per hour. This does not include the wear and tear on a vehicle. If you used the IRS mileage deduction of $0.555 per mile, at say, 40 miles per hour, and you come up with another $22.20 per hour for use of a police vehicle.

So, let's do a simple extrapolation of this single example. Take a small number, say 100 construction details going on at any point in time, 12 hours a day (and this is VERY conservative). At a cost of $62.20 per hour (excluding a lot of other costs related to operating a police "detail"), times 100 details, times 12 hours, times say 300 days per year, equals $22.4 million dollars. This is one use of government funds in one state for one single year.

By the way, this issue has been raised by numerous groups and individuals within our state in recent years. Supporters of the current method argue that the State Police details are no more costly than a "flagger". That is because certain political lobbies managed to get legislation passed in Massachusetts that sets a "minimum standard wage" for a "flagger" to more than $30 per hour in most cities and towns. Not sure about you, but I can't comprehend paying someone to stand up and wave a flag as much as a firefighter or a teacher or a local police officer. Politics at its finest...when you get a legitimate concern or complaint don't address it...just change the rules to make the concern invalid.

Now, do this exercise for every department of government that you interact with for a single day and see how quickly your blood boils. Above all, remember that this is YOUR money, the tax money that comes out of YOUR paychecks every week.

Here is another way to look at it... Let's say you make $1,000 per week, probably about $700 after taxes. Take the $300 that goes to the government and assume that 20% is wasted. Take that 20%, $60 per week times 52 weeks, and imagine $3,120 that should be in your pocket each year. Even if we only eliminated 10% of government waste...could you use another $1,560 in your pocket? Or, maybe we could balance the budget and start paying off our National Debt?

But then again, to discuss this waste means pointing fingers at specific self-interests funded by the government, and I wouldn't want to offend anyone...

What is the Point of All This?

Good question! As an individual citizen, particularly one that pays taxes, it is only natural, if not our responsibility, to demand to know "where is our money going?". Perhaps a better way to ask that same question is "what are we getting for our money?".

Regardless of anyone's particular "political persuasion", it is hard to argue that "government" is, at the very least, inefficient and bureaucratic. Many would argue that it is even worse than that, at least from a financial perspective, and that the government is inept and incompetent. And, unfortunately we have many examples of where our elected officials and their appointees have even proven to be corrupt and criminal.

So, what do we do? Hopefully you will continue reading...because there is a point to all this...even if it is somewhat rhetorical. At the very least, I hope you are doing what this has process has led me to do...which is to open my eyes even wider, ask more questions and to refuse to accept the status quo.

Chapter 4 – Bullets, Bandages and Smoke Screens

Regardless of whether they are effective or not, the politicians and the officials they appoint are certainly good at throwing money at problems...even if the problem is at the bottom of a wood chipper. All you have to do is look at the Federal Budget for the past few years (including the resulting Federal budget deficit) to see the immense amounts of money they spend. My favorite in recent years is what is referred to as "stimulus spending"...which has amounted to somewhere close to $2.0 TRILLION in the past 3-4 years. The question is - what did it stimulate?

Anyone that runs a company, big or small, will tell you there is a huge difference between "investment" and "overhead". Investment is made to create long-term value. Overhead is simply "the monthly bills". The problem with the "stimulus" is that, by all accounts, far more if it was thrown at "overhead" than "investment". Regardless of the necessity of some of these "overhead" expenditures, they provide little to stimulate long-term economic growth.

Take all the highway projects that have been started in recent years for example. Is there immense value in shoring up our infrastructure? Of course! Unfortunately, however, it does little to create long-term jobs. As soon as that highway is finished the people put to work in its construction are again unemployed. But then again, why should the politicians that allocated those funds care...they will be out of office collecting their lifetime pensions by then.

Conversely, if you built a factory to manufacture solar panels, a product the world is going to need for generations, you create jobs for as long as the factory is in operation. Just in case you were wondering, NO, we don't want the government in the manufacturing business. They can, however, subsidize the startup of certain key industries where private companies can then be more competitive in world markets.

When it comes to manufacturing in the U.S., there is another reality that cannot be ignored. Since U.S. consumers won't or can't pay above a certain level for many products, there is a limit to what manufacturing can be kept or brought back into the U.S. Take something as simple as a button-down shirt. For the sake of discussion, let's say that it takes 2 hours of labor to make that shirt. Even at minimum wage, the labor cost with taxes to make that shirt is close to $20.00...plus the cost of the material, plus the cost of the retailer's markup, plus the operating overheads of the retailer and the manufacturer, etc., etc., etc. Add that all up and that shirt, made in the U.S., will need to retail for at least $60.00 - $80.00. But what if people will only pay $20.00 for that shirt? It makes no sense to generate $80.00 in costs in for a product that can only generate $20.00 in income. The end result? The retailers and manufacturers go where the labor costs $2.00 for that same shirt. Sadly, for many products this is a reality that is unlikely to change.

For the U.S. to get back to solid, sustainable economic growth we have to put people to work in jobs that have long-term viability. To do that, we have to get back to manufacturing and in doing so address the trade deficit that has done so much damage over the past 20 years.

What I fear most is that the damage is much more extensive than we have realized, or that anyone will admit. I say this because there are certain industries and/or programs that have helped keep us from totally imploding in the last 10 years. Unfortunately however, these particular industries/programs, do not provide stable long-term jobs or build any foundation for the economy... I call them collectively the "the Bullets, the Bandages and the Smoke Screens"...

The Bullets...

It is only common sense to state (or re-state ad nauseam) that it is a good thing to keep manufacturing in the U.S. Ultimately, there are only a few "realities" that keep a particular manufacturing sector from going somewhere outside the U.S. where labor is cheaper..."logistical reality, "economic reality", "regulatory reality", etc.

For reasons of national security that are obvious, we as a country are not going to let factories in Asia or elsewhere build our military technology. So, while we would presumably never perpetuate two wars for more than 10 years for economic reasons, our economy has certainly benefited from them. Whether it be bullets or rifles, tanks or ships, the wars have by various accounts infused $1.0 - $2.0 TRILLION into the economy since they began. Many of the jobs maintained or added as a result of this spending are likely to be eliminated when the wars end. For this reason I consider the wars to have "artificially inflated" the U.S. economy during these "war years". Perhaps an even better way to describe this is to say that the wars have "artificially lessened the deflation" of the U.S. economy.

Like most elected officials, our current President was elected to occupy the White House based upon the promises he made to the American people. Among the key promises made in the 2005 campaign was to end our overseas wars and to bring our troops home. It is now 2013, 8 years later, and we are still deeply entrenched in conflicts in Iraq and Afghanistan. While there are plans in place to exit both countries, there is still a lot of evidence, if not propaganda, that neither place is yet able to maintain its own security. One thing is certain, there is far less being said by the White House these days about getting our soldiers home there than there was during the election season.

What is perhaps even more disturbing at the time of this writing is the situation in Syria. Although I should probably re-state that… What is more disturbing is what the White House IS SAYING about the situation in Syria… Our Commander in Chief is trying to justify a military attack on yet another foreign nation (it is late August 2013 as of this writing). Is all that has happened in Syria in recent years appalling? Of course!!!

But guess what…there are horrific things happening all over the world, every day, as has happened all over the world for centuries. Many of these happenings are at the hands of evil, corrupt and violent regimes. So why is the situation in Syria more compelling than any other? Good question…

The hard core "left" and "right" each have very strong positions on these topics. One side would probably accuse me (or my remarks) of being "insensitive"; the other "unpatriotic". Each would say that "These are complicated issues!", or "A lot is at stake!". I would argue with neither position. I am not going to use these pages to say that we should or shouldn't get into another military conflict. I am simply making the point that we do keep some people employed making all of the "hardware" that supports those conflicts. Sad but true…

I have promised throughout this book to try and minimize the political rhetoric…but there are some times when it is harder than others. I won't delve any deeper into discussions of the relationship between our military activities and our economy, with one exception. I will say that our primary fight should taking care of the people that live and work within our own borders.

The Bandages...

I don't use the word "bandages" in the traditional sense here, although in this context perhaps the word tourniquet would be more appropriate. In this case I am referring to the temporary/artificial measures put in place by the federal government to keep the economy from worsening or imploding. The problem with a tourniquet is that, as soon as you take it off, the bleeding starts again. Worse yet, you put the wounded tissue on the other side of the tourniquet in danger of dying permanently.

There are numerous things that can "stimulate the economy", from natural events to government intervention, aka, the ubiquitous "Economic Stimulus Package". These "packages" usually consist of "tax cuts" and/or "spending packages", each of which varies depending upon the timing and the agenda(s) of the "current administration".

Tax Cuts – The 1980s saw one of the first major use of tax cuts to stimulate the economy. It was a precursor to, if not the cause of one of the most prosperous decades in American history. The theory is simple – if people pay less in taxes, they have more to invest and/or spend, and that investment and spending infuses cash into the economy, which in turn creates growth. This approach does work, assuming the money saved by companies and individuals stays within the U.S. economy.

Spending Packages – It isn't unreasonable to assume that "government spending" will stimulate the economy, at least somewhat. The government buys "stuff" and "services", pays for them, and that money is infused into the economy. The problem is that these infusions seldom have a long-term impact.

Build a highway and you employ people until that highway is finished, after which they are then returned to the unemployment rolls. If those people, while employed, spend what they earn on imported goods, they in turn compound the trade deficit.

Government "spending packages" are almost never utilized to build or modernize factories, fund technological innovations (not directly anyway) or do anything else that creates or preserves long-term jobs. They do sound good in the media though.

Individual Government Supports – To list these programs by name would be tantamount to walking into a nuclear mine-field. There are many people in this country that legitimately and literally would die if they did not receive some form of public assistance. Anyone that would deny aid to someone that is legitimately unable to support themselves is inhuman. Unfortunately, however, there are many who CAN support themselves who choose not to. They make a conscious choice to live off "the system", in some cases making it a "family business" for generations.

It is one thing to need temporary assistance. My grandfather lost his small business in the Great Depression. He had no choice but to go to work for the WPA (the Works Progress Administration) to support my father and my grandmother. For 5 years he went to work every day with nothing more than a shovel, helping to build roads and bridges. Not once did he complain, even when his hands were raw and bleeding. He was not given an EBT card to purchase anything his heart desired; no cigarettes; no alcohol; no lobster... He received $5.00 a week plus coupons that could only be used for powdered milk, powdered eggs, flour, sugar and a few other "staples". My grandmother learned to turn these basics into delicious meals that we would give anything to have on our tables today. My grandfather never complained about his misfortune, never cast blame for his losses. He worked diligently and proudly for whatever he could make, every day until he died at age 84. I could not be more proud than to be his namesake.

At that desperate time in our nation's history there were those that, for whatever reason, did not choose to "pick up a shovel" and work for the WPA. They made their choice to "go on the dole" as it was known during that time. The "dole" was NOT a comfortable option...you moved to what was known as the "poor farm". These "poor farms" provided tents to live in and earth to grow food, a few other basics, but little more. You could survive, but that was it. It wasn't a "lifestyle"...it wasn't easy...and for most there was plenty of incentive to get back to work and back to EARNING some reasonable standard of living.

If we are going to help people who are struggling economically, then let's give them not a hand *out*, but a hand *up*..."teach a man to fish, don't just give a man a fish". Provide incentives to get off "the system"...and stop providing a comfortable "lifestyle" that makes it worth turning "the system" into a career.

The Smoke Screens...

The term smoke screen has traditionally been used to describe one action designed to hide another, or to describe statements designed to hide the truth, or perhaps to hide reality. A lot of statistics are used every day to "measure" and/or articulate the supposed "health" of our economy. The problem is that so many of these statistics are simply "feel good" numbers. They don't translate in any real way to an improved quality of life, much less a level of prosperity, for the average American citizen. Whether intentional, consequential or simply habit, the following "numbers" are reported regularly and are posited to measure the country's economic health. Personally consider I them meaningless and misleading.

Housing Starts – Traditional news media regularly report "things are looking up" by citing the number of new houses started under construction, aka "housing starts". On one hand it does show that we are building houses, which does creates some jobs (since we haven't started importing completely built houses from China yet). Unfortunately those jobs are temporary. We only keep those people at work as long as we need MORE houses. After all, you don't need more houses unless you have more people to put in them. All we have to do is have more children or let more people immigrate into the U.S. The problem is, we still don't have jobs for those people, so how are they to pay for those houses?

Interest Rates – This is another number that is confusing to most people. The fact is that interest rates change more as a result of current market trends than as a precursor of things to come. The Federal Reserve Bank, led by an appointee of the President of the United States, largely makes these decisions based upon his/her sole opinion of what is good for the economy. Unfortunately, as a political appointee, many would say this position can be readily influenced. Whether this is true or not, the Chairman of the Federal Reserve is the one that makes the decision to change the primary interest rates that are thought to either "stimulate" or "cool off" the economy.

For many years now, the "Fed" as it is also known, has kept interest rates incredibly low in an attempt to keep the economy moving, if not to keep it from collapsing. In theory, if interest rates are low people borrow and either spend or invest the proceeds (e.g. companies purchasing equipment), creating economic activity.

To effect that activity, however, banks must actually be willing to lend that money. Since the "mortgage crisis" that began in 2008, most people that have tried to borrow money will tell you that "you can't borrow money unless you don't need money".

One other "coincidence" (or maybe not) is that the Federal Government is in such debt that they are huge beneficiaries of these low interest rates. If interest rates were anywhere close to what they were in the 1970s practically the entire Federal Budget would be consumed by interest alone.

The Stock Market – Every day almost every news reporting agency in every form of media reports the "stock market" results, the theory being that these "market indexes" are an indicator of the health or future prospects of our economy. In point of fact, the major stock market indexes really only represent the health of certain companies and/or industries and don't typically translate directly to a change in the standard of living for the average American.

The reason for this is simple… To keep Wall Street "happy", publicly traded companies tend to focus almost singularly on immediate profits, in many cases with little regard for those they affect. One typical strategy for increasing these profits has been the elimination of domestic jobs, often in favor of overseas alternatives. In my opinion this bias towards profits makes them the farthest thing from an indicator of the standard of living in the U.S.

-   **The "Composite Index"** – A "composite index", at least as far as the "stock market" is considered, is the aggregate of the prices of the stock of a selected number of companies listed and sold on a particular stock exchange. The companies that make up this "index" are chosen because they are supposed to statistically represent the entire market's financial prospects, as indicated by the rise or fall of their collective stock prices.

The Dow Jones Industrial Average (the DJIA), for example, is a composite of the stock prices of 30 of the 2,800 companies traded on the New York Stock Exchange (the NYSE). If you totaled the revenue of all 2,800 companies traded on the Dow Jones, however, it would still represent only a small percentage of the overall U.S. economy. Yet for some reason we still use it as an economic barometer...

-    **Stock Price / the "Bottom Line"** – The "market value", i.e. the stock price, of a given publicly traded company is usually determined by the perceptions of the various investors that trade its stock. I use the term "perception" because stocks are bought and sold based upon speculation that the company will be worth more in the future. To be worth more in the future, at least as far as Wall Street is concerned, a company must have a high likelihood that it will become more profitable over time. The big question is HOW these companies drive that profitability?

Pick up any financial paper and you will read of X number of workers laid off or fired from company Y, resulting "in a one-time charge, Z improvement in their long-term earnings outlook, and an increase in their stock price to ZZ". This may be good for someone speculating on the growth of that stock, but too often that individual benefits at the expense of others.

From the standpoint of the AVERAGE citizen, growth in the stock market can mean financial gain or it can mean financial strain. If you are lucky enough to have had enough extra money to invest in the stock market (directly or via your retirement accounts), then your "fortunes" tend to increase as the stock market grows.

Today more and more Americans (if not most) work harder and harder every day just to make ends meet, leaving little or nothing to invest. For those people a booming or bullish stock market means nothing. It very likely means that they are struggling even more as so many companies enhance the value of their stock at the expense of their employees. It is their right as it is their money they are investing. What they fail to see, however, is that, if they keep laying off more and more people, sooner or later there will be nobody left to buy their products. What happens to the stock price then??

Gold & Oil Prices – it could be said that the past 8-10 years have represented a new "Gold Rush", during which time gold prices have increased almost fourfold! Many people have enjoyed very substantial profits riding this wave, however there is another very important aspect to this statistic.

Given that gold is a "commodity", like wheat and oil, oranges and pork bellies, it would be expected that its price would rise and fall according to fluctuations in supply and demand. And since the price of gold has been increasing, logic would suggest that one of two things has been happening – either supply has been shrinking or demand has been increasing. Let's assume for a moment that supply isn't the issue (by the way, it isn't...the world's gold supply is not in any jeopardy). So, is demand increasing?

Think about that for a minute...when and why do we buy gold? Personally we usually buy gold in the form of jewelry, something we do when times are good and when we have extra money. How many people do you know that are spending money on gold jewelry these days? Then there is the commercial market...gold is used in computers and electronics. Both of those industries have been flat for years along with the rest of the economy.

So if demand has not been increasing exponentially, why would gold cost so much more? It really isn't so much that gold is worth so much more, just that the dollar is worth so much less.

The U.S. was on the "gold standard" in one form or fashion until 1976. Under the gold standard the Federal Reserve had an equivalent value in gold stored away to back up every bit of currency in circulation (yes much if it in Fort Knox...). Once the gold standard was abandoned the value of a dollar became subject to a number of other influences, but I won't bore you with the details. I will just say that, to "stimulate" the economy, the Federal Reserve can "increase the money supply", essentially "printing more money". And the more "money" there is in circulation the less each dollar is worth. Think about it, if you cut a single pizza into 16 pieces instead of 8 pieces, do you really have more pizza?

The price of oil, e.g. a gallon of gas, heating oil, etc. is another indication of the value of the dollar. World oil consumption has not increased by multiples in the past ten years; however the price of gas has almost tripled in the same period of time.

So, if there haven't been any serious issues related to the supply of gold or oil in the past ten years, why would the prices of both have just about tripled? It isn't that they are worth three times more...it is because the dollar is worth 2/3 less.

New Unemployment Claims – as with the other employment-related statistics mentioned in Chapter 1, this statistic is misleading. A "new unemployment claim" can only be filed by someone that qualifies for unemployment, essentially someone that has been working. What about all those people that aren't working, that cannot qualify for unemployment??? What about those people that have exhausted their benefits??? Remember, we have more than 6.0 million people that want a job, that the government doesn't include in the "work force", and hence cannot collect unemployment.

While this statistic does indicate that fewer people are filing new claims to collect unemployment benefits, it says nothing about the overall employment situation in America because it does not include the increasing numbers of people that cannot qualify.

Distract and Deflect...

Another key tactic the government and/or the media use I will refer to as "distract and deflect". As I mentioned earlier, there is a great adage that seems to apply to even the most forthright politicians – "always tell the truth, just don't tell all of it". There is always an "issue of the day" that can be raised to keep us from focusing on the real issues that affect us.

On one hand this is somewhat understandable. If you keep saying "the world is ending" you cause panic and in turn increase the likelihood that the world will end. Maybe that is why the government and the media won't talk about the serious economic issues that are affecting real Americans every day. Maybe they are afraid that if people know how bad the economy really is they will panic and make it even worse. On the other hand, refusing to face our issues head-on is a major part of the reason they have gotten this bad.

So what do we do? First, we pressure our government officials and our media to talk about the real issue affecting us at home, and to stop talking about things overseas to keep us distracted. If our elected officials won't "get it together" throw them out of office and elect someone that will.

Bottom line – we all need to stare our issues in the face and solve them!

Chapter 5 – Other "Culprits"

In the course of writing this book I discovered that one of my greatest challenges was resisting the overwhelming temptation to play the "blame game". There is a fine line between attempting to identify the root cause of a given problem and just finding someone to blame. I was always taught to "blame the behavior", "not the person exhibiting the behavior", although if I could retrain myself to do the latter I would qualify for elected office... Sorry - couldn't resist.

Pursuing one's self-interest does not necessarily make someone a selfish person. That does not, however, mean that selfish people don't exist. And personally, I think selfishness and narcissism are at the root of so many of our societal and economic woes in this country.

You're probably saying "and your point is?" I'm not sure I know myself... What I do know is that there are those individuals and companies that continue to pursue their successes at the expense of others. This is perhaps another case of "which came first, the chicken or the egg?". So, as I attempt to identify some of the other "culprits" that have gotten us here, I will also attempt to present some causes and effects and you can draw your own conclusions.

The "Robber Barons"

Throughout the history of our country there have been a series of "robber barons", those that used the "lie, cheat & steal" school of business to get whatever they wanted. There were the "oil barons", the "steel barons", the "land barons", etc. In many cases we glorified them, choosing to call them "magnates", as it sounded more noble, or perhaps just less predatory.

We can look back to John D. Rockefeller, Andrew Carnegie, J.P. Morgan, etc., among so many other "pioneers" of American industry. They built huge companies that, in many cases, fueled the growth of the U.S. as a world economic power. They built the oil industry, the steel industry, the financial industry, industries that have employed millions of people for generations.

It would be callous to ignore all of the accomplishments of these and many other industrialists throughout the years. The companies they built have fed millions of American families. This does not, however make them saints. So many of them built their companies on the backs of the people that worked for them, most of whom worked for "survival wages". And while their employees suffered they themselves accumulated wealth beyond imagination.

This is not a condemnation of capitalism by any stretch. It is, however intended to point out a few individuals that have made their fortunes at the expense of others. Our capitalist "system", as well as our regulatory systems, have evolved to try and balance those interests. Countless labor laws and other regulations have been instituted to protect people from unsafe working conditions, parasitic wages, etc., many quite effective.

Creating laws and deploying regulatory agencies to enforce them only goes so far. We have numerous laws making it illegal to use, sell and/or manufacture illicit drugs. Yet, we still have a substantial drug problem in our country, because as long as people use drugs illegally, someone will find a way to supply them. The same applies to legitimate commercial industry. As long as we support the companies that prey upon us as members of the U.S. Economy, they will continue to play us as fools.

The "Real Estate Barons"

It is hard to pin down exactly when it happened, but sometime in the past 30-40 years the cost of real estate began to cripple our economy from within.

I remember growing up in the 1960s and early 1970s when my father, as a middle-class earner, could support a stay-at-home mother with four children. We had a modest but nice house and two used cars. We didn't have a lot, in fact very little by today's standards, but we didn't want for anything. All four of us kids found some kind of work to buy ourselves the little extras, raking leaves, shoveling snow, babysitting…anything that anyone would pay us to do.

As an adult, I purchased my first house in 1988, at a price equal to 4 times what my father paid for a house he purchased only 10 years earlier. These houses were, on the surface, identical in size, style and features. Again, I don't know what happened, but I do know that I really had to stretch to support this house as a single man. I would never have been able to support a family at the same time. And most everyone I know that has had a family since has required two incomes to be able to afford to own a house.

But I digress... While the cost of housing has becoming a painful fact of life in America, that isn't the point I am trying to make. As the cost of residential real estate has increased to outrageous levels, so has the cost of commercial real estate. It is my considered opinion that the companies that own, develop and manage commercial real estate are the "robber barons" of today.

Companies cannot exist without a place to conduct their business, whether it be manufacturing a product or retailing it, or simply managing it. While I won't bore you with the specific numbers, I will tell you that the cost increases for commercial real estate have far outpaced inflation throughout the past several decades. A few other important points to put this in perspective:

- To stay in business, companies must make a profit, or at the very least break even.

- Companies do not have endless supplies of money. Their "pie" can be cut into many pieces, but those pieces can still only add up to one pie.

- If the piece of the pie that pays "the rent" grows, other pieces must shrink. Those pieces include product cost, employee salaries, etc.

You may be asking yourself "what does this have to do with me?". The easiest way to explain this is to refer to that staple of American life – the "mall". Into this category, I'm going to lump the "big-box retailers, because they all occupy pretty much the same space. And that space cost a small fortune.

In 1998 a partner and I started a venture that involved renting a retail store-space in a strip mall; what would be today considered a "B-level" property. This 3,000 square feet space (50' x 60') cost us $7,200 per month, just for rent. That is $86,400 per year...in 1998...and it was not "prime" retail space.

Fast-forward fifteen years. Today, a retail store in a mall can cost anywhere from $50 to $100 per square foot, per year, depending upon the location. Take an average Abercrombie & Fitch store as an example. The one in my local mall is about 5,000 square feet in size. Do the math and they spend anywhere from $20,000 to $40,000 EVERY MONTH, just for rent.

How does a retailer like Abercrombie & Fitch pay that rent? First, they price a single pair of jeans from $78 to $98. Of course everything is "on sale" much of the time, so they seldom get those full prices. If you read their annual report you will discover that their "gross margin" averages almost 63%. Without detailed internal data, it is impossible to estimate their actual product cost for a single pair of their jeans. There are however numerous online resources available that will confirm a pair of jeans, while not Abercrombie & Fitch jeans, can be purchased from a Chinese manufacturer for anywhere from $5 to $10. A&F doesn't make their jeans in the U.S....you can draw your own conclusions.

I really don't have any particular "axe to grind" with Abercrombie & Fitch. They are simply one example of the thousands of different retail chains that have been "taken over the coals" by the real estate developers that rent them their space. They cannot possibly afford to manufacture their clothing in the U.S. AND pay their rent AND pay their employees AND make some level of profit to ensure that they stay in business.

As I said in a previous chapter, all you have to do is look at the labels on every product when you go shopping. See if you can even find something in a major retailer that is made in the U.S. today. Take it a step further...read the annual reports of companies with whom you do business. You may be amazed what you discover.

Apple

OK, I am going to pick on one company in particular. I'm not picking on Apple because I don't think they offer good products...they do. I'm not picking on them because they aren't a good company, because by many accounts, they are. People love their product and are fierce loyalists…and I'd be lying if I said I didn't love my iPod and my iPad…and iTunes as a service. I'm going to pick on them because I think Apple is glaring example of a company at the center of what is wrong with our economy; or maybe even with our society on the whole.

I apologize to any Apple loyalists that may be aghast at my making the company one of my "poster children", but I will explain (and as you can verify in their annual 10-K SEC filing for 2012).

- Apple did $156.5 BILLION in sales in 2012.

- Apple makes 100% of the devices they sell OVERSEAS.

- Their Cost of Goods (the cost to make the product they sell) was $87.8 BILLION in 2012; most, if not all of which went overseas.

- According to the company web site, Apple employs approximately 50,250 people in the U.S.

- Apple made a net profit in 2012 of $41.7 BILLION, which is 26.7% of sales!!!

These numbers are substantial; however they are meaningless without some context. It would seem like fairly straightforward exercise, pulling sales and income data for a few notable U.S. companies, and comparing that to the number of people they employ in the U.S. Or so I thought…

Believe it or not, very few companies openly publish the number of employees that they maintain in the U.S. any longer. Most are proud to publish their worldwide headcount, but embarrassed to declare their U.S. headcount. In 2010 even stalwart IBM stopped publishing the number of people they employ in the U.S.

So many companies aren't shy however, about declaring the number of people they are laying off. That is because Wall Street loves layoffs. It is astounding to me, if not infuriating, that so many U.S. companies are embarrassed to talk about the number of people they employ in their own home country. Perhaps even more importantly, they don't want anyone to know how many jobs they have shipped off-shore to "save a buck". I looked at dozens of annual reports just to cull out the U.S. employment numbers for the nine companies represented below.

What does it say that so many U.S. companies are ashamed to publish how many (or how few) people they employ in their own home country???

OK, back on track…and back to why I'm picking on Apple. First, let's compare Apple to a few other companies that operate in and out of the "tech sector" from the standpoint of sales versus U.S. employee count:

	Worldwide Sales (billons)	Net Income	% Sales	U.S. Employee Count	Sales per U.S. Employee (millions)
Technology Companies					
Motorola	$8.7	$0.88	10.13%	10,000	$0.87
IBM	$104.5	$16.60	15.89%	91,000	$1.15
Microsoft	$73.7	$16.98	23.03%	58,200	$1.27
Apple Computer	$156.5	$41.73	26.67%	52,500	$2.98
Other Industries					
McDonalds	$27.6	$5.47	19.82%	400,000	$0.07
Wal-Mart	$443.9	$15.70	3.54%	1,400,000	$0.32
Verizon Comm.	$115.8	$13.16	11.36%	170,162	$0.68
General Electric	$147.4	$13.64	9.26%	134,000	$1.10
Chrysler	$65.8	$1.67	2.54%	52,500	$1.25

Sources
Motorola - 2012 SEC 10K Annual Report, Corporate Responsibilities Report

IBM - 2012 SEC 10K Annual Report, U.S. Employees - IBM Employees Union Website
Microsoft - 2012 SEC 10K Annual Report, Web Site

Apple Computer - 2012 SEC 10K Annual Report

McDonalds - 2012 SEC 10K Annual Report

Wal-Mart - 2012 SEC 10K Annual Report

Verizon Communications - 2012 SEC 10K Annual Report

General Electric - 2012 SEC 10K Annual Report

Chrysler - 2012 SEC 10K Annual Report

Other Notes
Motorola - Employee Count is for North America (U.S. numbers unavailable)

Apple did $2.98 million in sales in 2012 for each of its employees. Another way to think of it is that it they only need ONE U.S. EMPLOYEE

to generate each $2.98 million in sales. The reason for this is simple –
they manufacture nothing in the U.S. They do keep thousands and
thousands of Chinese citizens working every day though...

This is just one reason why I am picking on Apple in these pages. The
second "sin" on my list is their stifling of innovation and/or their
unwillingness to "share the wealth". Until recently, if you wanted some
software or some accessory for your Apple computer or Apple device,
you had to buy it from Apple. When IBM introduced the first "IBM PC",
back in the early 1980s, they made it an "open" standard, encouraging
companies to make "IBM Compatible" software, computers, peripherals
and accessories. To this day consumers benefit from this openness. If
you have a PC, you have an almost infinite variety of companies from
which to buy your computer and/or expand your system's capabilities.
The "Apple world" is still largely controlled and limited by Apple, reducing
available choices for consumers and keeping prices artificially high.

The last, if not most important point I'll make pertaining to Apple is, in
some ways an off-handed compliment, but is at the same time a criticism
of our own consumerist society. Apple has done such an amazing job in
their product design, if not their marketing, that they have made their
products a "must-have" for every American adolescent. Let's face it, an
American teenager "will die" if they don't have an iPhone by age 12. Just
ask any teen or "tween" that you know... I stopped at a red-light a few
weeks ago and noticed four teenagers in a car next to me. All had
iPhones...all were texting...none talking to each other... I had to roll
down the window and ask them if they were texting each other? They
didn't seem to understand my point...

I grew up in a house with three sisters and two parents...we had one,
single phone line and one bathroom (and we walked to and from school
every day barefoot, in snow up to our waist, uphill both ways...☺).
Somehow we made it to adulthood without bearing the deep emotional
scars that parents today would inflict upon their children if they went so
far as to even take away their iPhone for a single day.

Wal-Mart

The next "demon" I will cite in this diatribe is, to me, one of the "worst of
the worst", in terms of contributing to the demise of the socio-economic

status of the average American. At the very least, they certainly take advantage of those in dire financial straits.

Whether positive or negative, there are many who have strong feelings about Wal-Mart. Mine relates to their outright **betrayal** of the American people. If you think the word betrayal is a bit harsh, consider the following. Sam Walton, Wal-Mart's founder used to take incredible pride in focusing their stores' assortment on products made in America. He and his company promoted that fact for many years, and used that Patriotism as a vehicle to build the company and its image.

At some point along the way they completely turned their back on American manufacturers and became one of the biggest companies in the world. I would challenge you to find even a handful of American-made products in their stores today. I will even go so far as to compare them to a "crack dealer" that "hooks" their suppliers and customers and takes over their lives.

If you are a large-scale marketer of consumer products, you have little choice but to sell to them. Once you do, their demands for rock-bottom product costs force you to take your production overseas. This also forces you to commit massive amounts of cash and other resources to manufacturing product for them...you are "hooked". And once you are hooked they push harder and harder until you barely make any money at all. This leaves nothing to develop other opportunities with other products or other customers. Finally, it puts you in a position that, if you lose them as a customer, you go out of business because of the overhead you created to support them.

As a consumer they "hook you" by convincing you that you can have everything you want. You get used to having a flat-panel TV in every room, etc. As soon as you (and your children) become accustomed to that lifestyle it is nearly impossible to go back. So when all of the "disposable" products they sell you break, die, etc., you have to go back to them for more of the same.

If you are unfortunate enough to have to work for Wal-Mart, you are then paid so little that you have no choice but to shop there as you cannot afford to shop anywhere else.

What is even more infuriating is that U.S. taxpayers are helping to support Wal-Mart's employees. There are numerous articles in the media that talk of high percentages of Wal-Mart workers receiving Medicaid, Food Stamps, and other "public assistance". This has been difficult, however to substantiate or quantify. The information available suggests that "the number" is somewhere between one third and one half of their U.S. Wal-Mart's.

This is not just a "Wal-Mart" issue...many companies pay wages that cannot support the everyday financial needs of an average family. What makes Wal-Mart the worst, in my opinion, is that they built their company on the backs of American workers and consumers, and turned their back on them. According to Wal-Mart's Annual Report, the company made a profit of $17 BILLION in the fiscal year that ended January 31, 2013, finishing the year with $7.8 BILLION in CASH in the bank. Yet they continue to pay their employees poverty level wages and buy the vast majority of the product they sell from overseas sources. Disgusting!!!

Chapter 6 – Can We Fix It?

I debate whether or not to call this chapter "How Do We Fix It?", but I am honestly not sure that we can. Things were much simpler and the country much smaller in the 1930s when my Grandfather went to work for the WPA. In many ways we are so spoiled in how we live today. Even in my very middle-class childhood in the 1960s and early 1970s, we had one TV, one phone, no computers, no cell phones, one car. By the end of the 1970's we somehow "needed more stuff", and Mom had to get a job, we had to get a second car, we stopped watching TV as a family.

Then it was the 1980s…we, the next generation of our family, were starting our careers, looking forward to new cars. In my case I remember the pride of buying an entry-level Rolex in 1986. Along the way I had lots of other "toys" and life experiences, and had a life not unlike many young executives in the "boom-boom '80s". It all seemed so easy…perhaps too easy?

The mid 90's brought for me a question, if not an epiphany. My mother died of breast cancer, and I didn't get to spend nearly as much time with her as I should have in her last years and months. I had been so busy chasing the next opportunity and the dollars associated with it that I lost sight of so much that is important in life. And in late 1994 I decided to make a change and walked away from an industry to which I had devoted much of my life for 13 years.

Following conventional wisdom I went back to school and earned a Master's degree, expecting that it would be a ticket to using my brains and experience more than my "blood and sweat". What I discovered after grad school was quite different, however. Companies were paying less and less and demanding more and more, leading to an unexpected life as an entrepreneur. It has been very rewarding and very educational on so many levels. It has not, however, been the path to riches and glamour that so many imagine when they envision the "life of an entrepreneur".

Like many of you, I have faced countless challenges building and trying to keep open a small company in an environment that seems to make it more difficult by the day. At the same time, I have seen countless friends and colleagues struggling to either stay employed or to find employment. Those that are employed have seen the pressures and stresses thrust upon them increase unabated. Those that have been "downsized", "laid off", etc. have had an impossible time finding work. I have a number of friends that are very talented, experienced and motivated that cannot even find a job in a retail store. Did I mention that they are over 45? Age discrimination is rife today! Recruiters are going so far as to tell them "off the record" that if they are even to get an interview they must "offer" to forego benefits, especially health insurance.

So, why do I tell you this? In part to "share your pain", assuming you've had similar experiences and frustrations in your own life and/or career. In part to explain why I'm not sure we can ever pull out of our economic "nose dive". It all boils down to selfishness, or perhaps whether or not we can achieve any level of selflessness. In "the interest of science" I will explore a couple scenarios…

Scenario 1 – If We Don't Fix It…

It was Albert Einstein that said "Insanity is doing the same thing over and over again but expecting different results.". Yet, we as a country do the same thing over and over again. It is hard to say "which is the chicken and which is the egg", the government or society at large. It is even harder to say which is in the best position to cure our economic ills. For the moment we will assume that it is neither…and explore a few aspects of American life if the current trends continue unabated.

Manufacturing – More and more companies will move more manufacturing overseas, wiping out even more skilled U.S. jobs. Our trade deficits will continue to accumulate, and we will owe foreign interests far more than the $8.0 TRILLION+ that we currently owe them.

Skills – As we move more and more manufacturing overseas, and furlough more and more skilled workers, we eventually lose those skills entirely. There are professions that survived for generations as the skills were passed on from the most experienced "craftsmen" to the newer "apprentices". Ask anyone under 30 years of age to describe the job of a "tool and die maker", a "tanner", a "pressman", etc. and see what answer you get.

When we went through our first "trade deficit driven" recession in the early 1990s a new term arose - "downsizing"; used to describe companies reducing their staff levels. Whether you call it "layoffs", "early retirement packages", "staff reassignments", etc., it meant people losing their jobs.

In earlier times, seniority was the rule; people with the least time on the job went first. In the 1990s this changed with the arrival of the "early retirement package", the rationale being the reduction of the "most costly" employees. In the end, many, many companies simply accelerated their own demise, because they gave up the employees with the most experience, perhaps those with the experience to get the company through the tough times.

Jobs – With an even smaller manufacturing base in the U.S. there will be even fewer "skilled jobs" available, and to survive people will have to take on lesser positions or change professions. Regardless of how the government chooses to report it, more people will be unemployed or underemployed.

Wages – With fewer "skilled jobs" available, and more people seeking employment, people will have to accept pay cuts in order to find any work at all. "Wage deflation" has been a fact of life for many people for years already.

Many are outraged by the wages offered for the few jobs that are available, that often tend to be in the retail or the service industries. Out of pure self-interest, if not survival instinct, these people and others lobby for an increase in the "Minimum Wage" thinking that will solve the problem.

Those that think increasing the Minimum Wage is a "good thing" are ignoring reality, human nature or both. Many companies are already "on the brink", struggling just to keep the doors open while barely breaking even or losing money, doing everything they can to try and survive the recent recessions. These are the companies that will go out of business if they are forced to pay higher wages. Remember the Twinkie???

Then there are the companies that have been trying to keep jobs here in the U.S...that will finally be forced to send even more jobs off-shore. We as consumers go elsewhere when we cannot afford to pay a particular seller's price. Why should a company behave any differently?

Mandating a higher Minimum Wage only will increase wages for those that currently earn Minimum Wage. For companies that have no choice but to pay Minimum Wage to stay afloat this will mean either reducing staff levels or going out of business. Either way it just puts even more people out on the street...

As a small business owner who has lived through these scenarios for 15 years, I can promise you this will happen. I say this not as a threat, but an acknowledgement of reality...you cannot give people money that is not there.

Interest Rates – With fewer companies making a profit, higher unemployment, and working people paid lower wages, the tax income that the government relies on to operate will be reduced. With a lower tax base the government will have to borrow more, increasing the national debt. Sooner or later, that debt load will make it riskier for the investment markets and foreign governments to lend money to the U.S. government. Sooner or later that increased risk will translate into higher interest rates. Higher interest rates will increase the percentage of the Federal Budget that goes towards interest (currently $200 billion per year). As the government's interest bill increases, its ability to spend money to stimulate the economy will decrease, exacerbating the problem further, if not exponentially.

Scenario 2 – If We Somehow Find a Way to Fix It...

It would be less than truthful to tell you that I believe we can fix our economy to a level where it isn't continuing its downward slide (even if at a reduced rate of decline), much less restore some level of prosperity. In the interest of science, if not as a display of my optimistic nature, I will attempt to portray at least one scenario that illustrates a positive outcome. Unfortunately there are a lot of "ifs" that will need to become reality in this scenario, but again I will try to create a utopian view.

Investments in Industry – Under this scenario, through a combination of corporate tax incentives and government grants, new factories are built and existing factories are modernized. Using technology and automation, high levels of productivity are created, making it more feasible to pay higher wages to those the factories can employ. At the same time, this efficiency will make U.S. companies more competitive, reducing foreign competition and helping to reduce the trade deficit. And of course, with increased revenue (and presumably profits) flowing through U.S. companies, the government increases its tax revenue and improves its own financial capabilities.

Investments in Education – The government will accept the fact that not all citizens are able to learn and contribute on an equal level and eliminate programs like "No Child Left Behind" that are failing miserably in their intent. Instead of "dumbing down" everything so that everyone can pass, new programs will help individuals maximize their opportunities based upon an education focused on their specific interests, abilities and aptitudes. This will generate a much more confident work force that is oriented to the individual strengths of its members.

Tariffs & Import Taxes – Many economic scientists will cringe at even the mention of import taxes and tariffs. They will argue that this is "protectionist" and will hinder a "free market economy", ultimately damaging our economy. The problem with this "science" is that we are NOT in a "free market". When I think of a pure "free market" I think of a market where everyone plays by the same rules, and fair competition ensures equal opportunity for all. If you apply the "pure science" over time, eventually everything equalizes and everyone benefits.

Let's see what happens if we try to "equalize" things between an American worker and a Chinese worker. According to a variety of sources (hard data is hard to come by), the AVERAGE Chinese worker makes approximately $650 a month, $7,800 a year. A MINUMUM WAGE American worker makes $1,256 a month, $15,080 a year. An AVERAGE American worker makes over $40,000 per year (U.S. Bureau of Labor Statistics). Not sure how we could equalize things, but I am sure that we in the U.S. cannot afford to decrease our wages to a level anywhere close to the Chinese. And the government regulated wages in China are unlikely to rise to our levels.

By instituting tariffs on products coming from countries where a trade deficit exists we make it somewhat more feasible to compete. At the very least, we generate BILLIONS of dollars in tariff revenue that the government can use to balance the budget and to reinvest in our own industries.

Wages & Compensation – Increasingly, companies will realize that their employees are partners in their success. They will realize that investing in employees actually contributes to growth and profitability. They will provide profit sharing and other incentives that motivate employees to make the company more successful. And they will invest in the education of their employees to increase their skills and their ability to contribute.

This "partnership" type of relationship between companies and their employees will lead to better total income for workers. It will also lead to a more secure working environment as companies will be focusing more on long-term investment and innovation than they will be on short-term profits.

Interest Rates & Borrowing – Interest rates will be kept low because the government will reduce waste and get its spending under control. Ultimately, interest rates are stabilized and kept low and a balanced budget is achieved.

This is not the only factor. In the private sector money must actually be loaned and put in the hands of those who can turn it into investments and ultimately into profits that perpetuate further investment and growth. When the government provides loan guarantees that make it EASIER and FASTER for businesses to borrow money, it is certain to create more jobs...

Inflation – Between the combination of U.S. economic growth and new tariffs increasing the cost of imported goods, prices are likely to increase. While many would say "we cannot afford it", that is a knee-jerk reaction. We have been "affording it" for a long time…wages decreasing…fuel and other prices increasing, etc. The bottom line is that, with higher prices, we will think twice about what we purchase, pay for only what we really need, shop for products of great quality as well as great value - and perhaps stop filling our landfills with junk.

Real Prosperity – REAL long-term prosperity means that people's lives are improved on ALL levels. This means people are able to pay their bills without using their credit cards. It means people are saving money at a level sufficient to fund their retirements. It means our educational system is creating motivated, talented, creative people, prepared to make contributions to society, intellectually and financially.

Chapter 7 – A Few More Ideas...

I would again lose my claim to being an "eternal optimist" if I didn't at least make an attempt to put forth as many ideas as I could to improve things. Giving up has never been in the American vocabulary, nor is it in mine.

To some, these ideas may seem radical or outdated or unrealistic. To those individuals I would say simply, "Why? How much worse could they make things than they are now?". Regardless of anyone's political convictions, we all have a part in this and will all be affected more and more if we don't turn things around.

The current "system" upon which we base our economy, and to a large extent our society, is not working, and hasn't been working for more than 20 years! We keep trying to tell ourselves that "things will get better...they have to get better"...but they don't. We put "bandages" on things, we rationalize, we do "more of the same"...and it stays the same.

So maybe it is time for some radical new ideas, or at least to implement some radical old ideas. I may repeat a few concepts mentioned in previous pages, but this is because I believe these are concepts, if not programs that need to be put in place if we are ever to recover.

Convert Hand-Outs to Hand-Ups

Someone very much wiser than I once said, "Give a man a fish and you feed him for a day...teach a man to fish and you feed him for a lifetime...". The W.P.A. (Works Progress Administration) gave people a way to survive when things became desperate in our country, eventually helping the U.S. work itself out of the Great Depression. The W.P.A. offered simple jobs that compensated people with basic sustenance who had no other options. By giving them just the basics it also gave them plenty of incentive to work hard to find something better. It was a major force in helping the U.S. to extract itself from the clutches of the some of the darkest days in U.S. History.

Sustenance, NOT Lifestyle – Many states, like my home state of Massachusetts, make life on its welfare program so comfortable that it becomes a family business, passed on from generation to generation. A recent study published by the Cato Institute (*The Work versus Welfare Trade-Off: 2013, by Michael D. Tanner and Charles Hughes*), illustrates glaringly that it is more lucrative to stay on public assistance than it is to work. According to the study, Massachusetts (which is, believe it or not only the third worst state in the country in this regard), the value of welfare benefits adds up to pre-tax dollars of $42,515. Someone making minimum wage, working 40 hours for 52 weeks makes $15,080. The incentive to get off welfare is…what???

Opponents of welfare reform come up with every possible excuse…child care is unaffordable, jobs are unavailable, etc. As a taxpayer it is pretty difficult not to respond to those excuses with anything but an expletive…but I will refrain. My censored answer to that retort is "That is the response I would expect from those who are either lazy, corrupt, unimaginative or all of the above!". Sorry but this is an emotional topic!

Here is what you do… You convert all welfare to "workfare"…if someone gets a check they make SOME contribution to society, for example:

- Put some of the people that are on welfare to work running daycare centers to free up other "workfare" people to work.

- Everyone works…cleaning public buildings, cleaning streets, building roads, stuffing envelopes, etc.

- If you aren't working, you are studying at a supervised facility, acquiring whatever skills, credentials, degrees, etc. it takes to qualify for a job.

- No more "universal" cash benefits, food stamps, EBT cards, etc. Benefits will be specifically restricted to BASIC needs…not alcohol, tobacco, lottery tickets, etc.

- Housing is provided by voucher, not cash, and it is basic housing, not luxury condos.

Citizenship by Service – Billions of dollars trade hands every day in the U.S. in the "underground economy" that exists for people that don't or can't exist legally in within our borders. Many of these people do so for reasons of desperation…the jobs and "safety nets" simply don't exist the in their homelands. They come here to earn a living, to support their families and many work incredibly hard. Personally I would rather find a way to legitimize several million "undocumented workers" who work their butts off than continue to support an equivalent amount collecting a check sitting on the couch. If someone wants to be here to work, let's give them an opportunity to contribute to society in some capacity and EARN citizenship.

- Provide day/week visas for "day-laborers" who will work at jobs that in many cases American workers won't accept.

- Provide for a lower minimum wage for migrant day-laborers, augmented by dormitory housing and transportation from the border. This will provide a lower cash cost for certain industries, e.g. farming, that currently use undocumented workers for lack of any other options. By the way, we then can collect some taxes on those wages.

- Give citizenship to any "day laborer" that works for a period of time, say 2 years, paying taxes (and of course meeting the other educational requirements to qualify for citizenship).

- Allow immigrants to serve in the American military, earning citizenship if they earn an honorable discharge.

- Create a Public Service Corps., providing W.P.A. level benefits and housing to immigrants as a path to earning citizenship. This work force can build roads, fix bridges, clean cities and towns.

Protect Innovation

As we discussed in earlier pages, our system of intellectual property protection (the USPTO the (U.S. Patent & Trademark Office) and the laws that support it) needs to be overhauled. Innovation and invention has been one of the key "fuels" driving our economy for almost as long as the U.S. has been in existence. If we don't do a much better job of protecting what we create, as individuals and as companies, we lose any remaining incentive to "go the extra mile". Why "kill ourselves" building a product or a company if someone else is going to steal our idea and capitalize on it at our expense.

For those of you that aren't totally familiar, there are a number of different classifications of "intellectual property". In the simplest of terms, patents are intended to protect "inventions", trademarks to protect "identification" and copyrights to protect "art". I'll explore each briefly, lest I go off on a tangent that would be as interesting to read as it would be to watch the grass grow.

Patents were once a great source of protection and a great source of pride for an inventor. Inventions like the light bulb and the telephone are as much parts of American history as they were innovative devices patented by their inventor.

An argument could be made today that much of what can be invented has been invented. If that is the case, we are still left with the opportunity to innovate what has already been invented, and those innovations can be patented. Unfortunately with more than 9,000,000 patents having been issued, we may even be starting to run out of potentially unique innovations.

Not really, but it has become harder and harder to patent anything new. For fear of a new patent infringing an existing patent on some level, new applications are rejected over and over until they are so narrow that they protect virtually nothing. Compounding matters, the claims made in a patent application are exposed as soon as they are filed. This immediately gives competitors the time and insight to circumvent them.

Moving away from patents, we also have trademark and copyright protections available to us. A trademark, much like a person's signature, identifies a company or a product. Taking the form of a unique word or image, a "trademarked" property is more easily protectable, providing that it does not infringe the "mark" of another person, entity, company, etc. Copyrights are even a bit simpler, in that a work of art (e.g. a book, music, painting, etc.) is protectable at the moment of its creation, again as long as it is not a copy of another existing work.

The unfortunate "fact of life" for all intellectual property is that it only has value if you have the money to defend it. This may seem ludicrous, if not outrageous, but every day companies copy products and violate patents, trademarks and copyrights, something I have experienced personally. Confront these companies and the response is "ok, so what…go ahead and sue us….if you can.". The cost of defending any form of intellectual property is at minimum tens of thousands of dollars…in some cases hundreds of thousands of dollars…and it can take many years.

Interested in a cautionary tale? Look up Robert Kearns, the inventor of the intermittent windshield wiper, and his battle with Ford Motor Company. Outrageous as it is, what happened to Mr. Kearns happens every day.

But I digress...the point I am trying to make is that we need a better, faster, simpler and more effective method of protecting intellectual property. The following would be a good start.

Documentation of Creation – The USPTO, at one time, had a program whereby an inventor could mail in documentation of an invention to establish an invention date. This gave an inventor time to properly protect his invention. Unfortunately this program was discontinued in 2007. Whether it be a patent or any other "creation", there needs to be a system to document and to protect the "first creator".

There is also another common-law protection called "trade dress" that is meant to protect a product design and its creator. This protection needs to be strengthened and reinforced. Today companies, particularly large retailers, steal product designs with impunity.

Defense & Prosecution – Today the only recourse for someone whose intellectual property has been "misappropriated" is a lengthy, expensive lawsuit. This misappropriation is often very obvious and easy to document.

There needs to be a fast and easy means of filing a complaint and securing an injunction to stop such instances of infringement. If certain REASONABLE standards are met, the creator should have costs associated with the defense of his/her property covered.

Making these offenses criminal as well as civil would be another effective deterrent. There are many for whom price-fixing and other anti-trust law violations have secured jail terms. Theft of intellectual property is equally (if not more) damaging to U.S. markets and should be prosecuted as energetically. Company executives will be far more hesitant to violate other people's intellectual property if they know a prison term can result from their actions.

Availability of Capital

Money is one of those things in life...the more you need it the less likely you are to get your hands on it. Countless businesses and products, often GREAT businesses and products, die because there is simply not enough money to see them through to fruition.

Most entrepreneurs will tell you that it takes 3-5 years for a single venture to get to the point of profitability. They will also tell you that single venture will burn through 2-3 times more cash than was ever imagined when the venture was started. The problem is, without the profits, or the assets that those profits purchase, the venture has no borrowing power. Many entrepreneurs exhaust every penny they personally have or can borrow just to get the venture off the ground. When they run out of money they are left with no choice but to get a job or move on to something else.

Capital must be AVAILABLE to those that need it. Why do businesses typically need money (besides operating cash)? They need it to buy equipment, to design a new product or fund its production, to secure a patent, etc. During difficult economic times, every dime is often required to just keep the doors open. There is nothing left to invest in the new opportunities that can mitigate economic downturns and/or lead to more prosperous times. This does not mean "opening the floodgates" and giving money to anyone that asks. It means providing capital for responsible use:

- **Loans/Loan Guarantees** – This is not to suggest for a moment that we keep the SBA alive. I am suggesting, however that some form of government loan guarantees be given to qualified businesses. In today's market a "qualified business" generally has enough collateral to mitigate the need for a guarantee. This needs to be changed so that guarantees can be obtained based upon a reasonable business plan. This plan should show that the funds are going to develop a new opportunity that, if realized, has a reasonable probability of repaying the loan. There has to be some acceptance of risk, by the government and the banks, if funds are going to be matched up with opportunities.

- **Capital Grants** – Countless companies could develop new opportunities and create new jobs if they had the capital to invest in new equipment. Besides the jobs created operating the new equipment there is a "trickle-down" whereby it creates jobs throughout the supply chain that produces that equipment.

The government should initiate a program whereby a company can apply for and receive a capital grant to be utilized to buy equipment manufactured in the U.S. The qualifications for these grants should also include hiring of new employees to operate this equipment. If the company doesn't prove this hiring and continued maintenance of the new jobs, they repay the money.

This program should also apply to existing industries where the opportunity to modernize facilities exists, and would result in new domestic jobs.

- **Seed Money** – Another program that would bear fruit is one that provides the initial start-up capital to fund a new venture, assuming it can demonstrate potential. This potential can be demonstrated by the development of certain intellectual property, for example securing a patent. It could also include funds necessary to produce a new product or service for which an order has been secured.

- **Tax Credits for Capital Investment** – Give larger companies SUBSTANTIAL incentives to invest in equipment that creates jobs in the U.S. This would seem to be painfully obvious, but it doesn't get done. Countless companies keep BILLIONS of dollars in their "overseas subsidiaries" to avoid the onerous domestic taxes. We can demonize them for doing so, but as individuals we don't want to pay more taxes than we have to...so why should companies? You get "more flies with honey than vinegar"...so let's give those with money good reason to invest it in US, in the U.S.

Invest in "Industry Supportive" Infrastructure

In addition to providing capital to fund operations and development within individual companies, the government should be investing in the infrastructure to support them. This infrastructure should improve the reliability and lower the costs associated with operating a company in the U.S. Some of these improvements should include:

- **Rebuild the Electrical Grid** – The network of electrical wiring and interconnections across the U.S. has long been outdated and inefficient. In some cases, "the grid" has gotten to the point of either being so overloaded or so "broken down" that it has become increasingly unreliable. The government should be funding the upgrade and replacement of the infrastructure via grants to the existing providers. This would of course require a level of accountability whereby these grants are proven to increase BOTH reliability AND efficiency. This will make the "grid" more dependable while at the same time lowering the cost of delivery, and in turn the cost of electricity.

- **Solar Farms** – Arguably there is no more dependable source of electricity than the sun. If we just took the money the government wastes each year and spent it building solar farms we would have 100% of our electricity coming from clean sources at a fraction of what it costs today. Of course the equipment to build these farms must be made in the U.S. Even it if is more expensive it still pays for itself many times over.

- **Connectivity & Communication** – A case could easily be made that the availability, performance and reliability of the Internet is critical to the long-term health of our economy. It facilitates many aspects of business; it is becoming a conduit to educating our populace; and in a real way it connects us to the rest of the world. It is not unreasonable to suggest that a portion of our tax dollars be invested to ensure its reliability and availability to all. This is being done to a certain extent, for example free cell phones to economically disenfranchised individuals, but not to businesses.

- **Upgrade and Update our Highways & Bridges** – This is a "no-brainer"…everyone knows our bridges and highways are in terrible shape. The problem here is the "insanity" of our current approach. We continue to use the same materials and technologies that have proven not to last. The cost of not repairing our infrastructure is more often compounded by the increased traffic and disruption to society that those repairs cause. We MUST start building things that last and can be maintained with less disruption!

- **Alternate Transportation** – While we do need to update and improve our roads and bridges, we also need to reduce the load on them. We need to continue to develop rail systems and other means of transportation that will take advantage of these inexpensive new electrical resources to move our people and our goods around the country.

- **Water Distribution System** – Whether you believe "global warming" is a real phenomenon or not, one thing is for sure – our weather patterns have become more severe and more erratic. Add to that the increased threats of contamination to our water supply from "modern life", and water is going to become our most precious, if not our most endangered resource. Droughts plague different parts of the country at different times, as do deluges of rain and floods. We need to be able to capture, store distribute clean water across the country as needed to ensure that our most critical resource is available where it is needed, when it is needed. We have an electrical "grid" and a communications "grid" (the Internet)…why not a water "grid"?

Stop the Political Lunacy

Many share my opinion that our political process is broken. Whether it is broken beyond repair remains to be seen. Once thing is certain - things need to change in a major way to force the government to get back to SERVING the populace as was intended by our Founding Fathers, and not the other way around.

Election Reform – There is little today to prevent special interests from buying candidates. This isn't to say that all elected officials are corrupt, or willingly "sell" their votes to a constituent or group. However, the current election process favors candidates who can afford to travel and advertise widely to get their message to potential voters. Special interests fund political campaigns through PACs (Political Action Committees), who use those funds to influence which candidates are "pushed". The end result is that we as individual citizens only get the opportunity to vote for candidates that the special interests have selected. Those that don't "toe the party line" or make the "right promises" don't get funded and we never get to know them. If this is ever going to change, we need major election reform. A few particular suggestions:

- **Make PAC's Illegal** – Restrict campaign contributions to DIRECT contributions, making it illegal to "funnel" them through PACs or any other means of creating influence.

- **Make Lobbying Illegal** – Eliminate the ability of special interests to "sell" our elected officials on voting a certain way. Our officials should be voting based upon OBJECTIVE information that they garner for themselves, from their constituents, not from those that can afford to park themselves outside the offices on Capitol Hill.

- **Fund a Third Political Party** – Our country's "two party system" is largely why our political system is so polarized, if not paralyzed. Each party has gotten so extreme in the interest of being opposed to the other that a balanced, moderate point of view has all but disappeared in government.

- **Distribute Campaign Funds Equally** – Rather than allowing direct contributions to any party, have them all put into a single pool, that pools to be distributed equally amongst parties that can demonstrate at least a modicum of public support. This will ensure that all points of view, i.e. all political platforms, are given an equal opportunity to present themselves to the public.

- **Eliminate the Electoral College** – There is no longer any reason for us to not use that Popular Vote. The vote of ALL CITIZENS should determine who is elected to the offices that largely determine our fate.

Force the Government to Spend Responsibly – The government, e.g. Congress and the White House, create and pass the annual budgets that determine how much money is spent for what. If we had a "Balanced Budget Amendment" they could not spend more than they take in, but we do not. Our government has borrowed and borrowed and borrowed…and mortgaged the futures of our children and grandchildren.

Sooner or later they will have to stop borrowing and stop over-spending, but they aren't going to do it on their own - we have to force them. One way to force them is by limiting the taxes they can collect from us. I am not suggesting to anyone that they NOT pay their fair share of their taxes. I am suggesting however that every American pay no more than what is absolutely fair, necessary and legally justifiable:

- **Save EVERY Receipt** – The list of items which are tax-deductible changes every year. Don't believe me? Try this: save every receipt for a year and make notes right on it what it was for...gas to go to a training seminar, over-the-counter medication, books to develop a new skill for work, dinner with a business associate, etc. At the end of the year categorize them and total them up, then give them to your tax preparer. You may be surprised what you can save in taxes, particularly when you can document it.

- **Keep a Mileage Log** – Believe it or not there are a lot of trips that we make for which the mileage is tax deductible. Driving to school to pursue certain types of education, trips for medical treatment, driving to a second job, or driving related to your work that isn't commuting back and forth. Keep a log of every mile you drive and the purpose of each trip and you may be surprised. Again, consult your tax professional.

- **Cut Your Spending/Start Saving** –We all have to be more responsible and do more to put money aside for emergencies, major purchases, retirement, etc. Not only that; by not spending your hard-earned dollars, you deprive the government of the revenue it generates from sales taxes. Sales taxes in 37 states, income taxes on the profits from every company associated with your purchase, etc...it all adds up very quickly.

- **When You Spend, Spend on Tax Deductible Items** – Consult with your tax preparer to find out expenditures are tax deductible in your particular situation. You'll be surprised to learn which educational, business and medical expenses can be deducted - not to mention certain retirement investments. Put your money into those things instead of into unnecessary "stuff". You will save money on taxes and likely enrich your life in the process.

Replace Obamacare – The intent of Obamacare is noble - to ensure that all Americans have health care. The problem is that this program was developed and shoved down America's throat with virtually no forethought. The program has so many elements that simply ignore common sense, human nature or both.

The current iteration of "Affordable Health Care Act" forces companies to give paid health insurance to employees working more than 32 hours. The end result? Companies, especially those that cannot afford it, are simply going to cut hours below 32, or eliminate positions entirely. Imagine the following conversation:

> **John** – "Hey Mary, guess what? Thanks to Obamacare I am getting free health care!"

> **Mary** – "That's good news…but I thought you were laid off?"

> **John** – "I was, but I still get it"

> **Mary** – "Why were you laid off?"

> **John** – "Because my company couldn't afford to pay for Obamacare."

This conversation is going to play out many thousands of times in the next few years if this program is not restructured or eliminated. It cuts into the paychecks of people that are already struggling to survive. Obamacare actually does more to hurt the people it is intended to help than if the government did nothing at all.

All the White House would have had to do is talk to business owners and the program could have been made more viable from the very start. But since when did politicians ever listen to their constituents…after all voters don't finance campaigns…

Buy American...

Whenever you make a purchase, however small, look at the packaging and find out where it is made. You will likely be shocked when you realize how few "Made in the U.S.A." options you have in your day-to-day purchases. So, what choice do you have then?

- **Don't Buy** – Unless it is something you absolutely NEED (not want), pass until you find something that is made in the U.S.A.

- **Avoid Big Box Retailers** – The biggest of the retailers are the biggest offenders when it comes to buying product made outside our borders.

- **Shop Online and in Local Specialty Retailers** – The small "Mom & Pop" shops oftentimes work with the "boutique" manufacturers that still exist in this country. Many of these "second tier" manufacturers that aren't supported by the "Big Boxes" also turn to online retailers and marketplaces to sell their products.
- **Understand the Different "Made in the USA" Language** – just because a product says "Made in the USA" doesn't mean it is made entirely in the USA. It may just be assembled in the USA, or it may be made in the USA from overseas materials. Look up the manufacturer and find out just how much they actually do here in the U.S., or at least how many people they employ here.

Stop Using Cash...

The tougher things have gotten the more ways the government has found to make sure they get their money from you. New regulations have made it necessary for every company to have a tax form on file identifying the taxpayer information for every single entity with which they do business. This makes it possible to report where every single dime a company spends goes. It could then be cross-referenced with every company (or individual receiving a 1099) declaring income. I can't wait for that to be required…business owners will be spending half their day just doing government required paperwork. Not that the government shouldn't be able to collect all of the taxes to which it is entitled. It just shouldn't be so burdensome that we aren't left with the time to run our businesses.

Taxes are a fact of life, and are necessary to keep our government functioning, which unfortunately is necessary to keep our society functioning on some level. The issue I have personally is that there is nothing necessitating that those "powers that be" act responsibly. It is up to us as citizens to hold our government officials accountable. How do we do that? One, we vote those out of office that do not respond to the real needs of the population as a whole. And two, through our actions we force them to act. If we find ways to support ourselves through non-taxable means we reduce the available tax dollars that they "play with".

Barter – this has long been a means of generating "value" for oneself that flies "under the radar". The government does not let us write off as tax deductible any time we spend doing charitable work. It can therefore be inferred that our time is "valueless" from a cash perspective, unless we actually collect cash for it. So, if we trade our time for someone else's time, no cash changes hands, thus no tax implication is created. It is simply one person helping another and them returning the favor.

There are a number of web sites that are starting to make it even easier to find those looking to "exchange favors". Just do a quick web search for "barter my time"...you will be surprised how easy it is.

Feed Ourselves...

More and more individuals are growing their own food in their own gardens. And many cities and towns have "community gardens" where people can use fertile land to grow their own produce. What better way to get good, fresh, organic food at the lowest possible cost.

Coupons – countless companies make coupons available on a daily basis. This is a very easy way to keep more money in our pockets and reduce sales taxes paid to the government.

Barter – again, trade off food and other household basics that we can produce ourselves with neighbors that produce other goods.

And This is Just the Start...

These are just a few of my own personal ideas. There are many people out there that are smarter and more creative than me. And there are plenty of other great ideas out there. But we dismiss them because they are not "politically correct" or because "we've never done it that way before". This may be idiotic, but it is also human nature.

We have to be BRAVE and DETERMINED and we have to think "out of the box". We have to be willing to try new things and to give them the support that they need. And we have to give them time to work.

So...what are your ideas??? And what are you doing to turn them into reality???

Chapter 8 - Where Do We Go From Here?

We are all in this together, all 316,558,116 (at this exact moment) of us that live in the United States of America. So, how do we "right the ship"?

Look in the Mirror

I found a small plastic "gadget" one day, a little bigger than a wallet. It had a quote on the cover – "**the solution to our problems lies within**". I opened it up…it was a **mirror**.

It is easy to say "I'm only one person, what can I do?". That is nothing but a "cop out"! If our Founding Fathers thought that way we would all still be speaking with a British Accent. One of my favorite quotes has been attributed to various sources, in various forms, from Plato to Edmund Burke.

"All that is necessary for the triumph of evil is that good men do nothing"

One person can make a difference! It means refusing to accept the "status quo" and it means taking whatever actions, however small, diligently and with determination.

In 1776 a handful of determined, patriotic individuals banded together and refused to accept a status quo that did not represent the interests of the people. These men built a country…what are you going to do???

Additional Exhibits & Other Resources

Top Trade Deficit Nations – 1992-2012

Country	Imports (millions)	Exports (millions)	Cumulative Surplus/ (Deficit)
China	$3,761,976	$813,127	($2,948,849)
Japan	$2,641,663	$1,228,073	($1,413,590)
Canada	$4,704,423	$3,885,313	($819,110)
Mexico	$2,989,250	$2,239,093	($750,157)
Germany	$1,365,419	$698,209	($667,210)
Venezuela	$477,838	$153,222	($324,616)
Italy	$524,978	$232,645	($292,334)
Nigeria	$318,024	$39,811	($278,213)
Saudi Arabia	$454,150	$178,425	($275,725)
Ireland	$406,115	$131,542	($274,572)
Malaysia	$486,587	$215,062	($271,525)
Taiwan	$700,602	$433,730	($266,872)
Thailand	$349,456	$143,985	($205,471)
South Korea	$761,884	$568,759	($193,125)
France	$613,139	$433,320	($179,819)
Russia	$259,489	$91,012	($168,477)
Indonesia	$232,756	$80,432	($152,324)
India	$328,820	$176,629	($152,191)
Iraq	$145,961	$15,823	($130,138)
Algeria	$147,329	$20,735	($126,594)
Angola	$133,913	$15,191	($118,722)
Sweden	$196,077	$80,492	($115,585)
Israel	$280,130	$181,246	($98,884)
Vietnam	$119,873	$28,465	($91,408)
Norway	$108,520	$43,021	($65,499)
Total 1992-2012	$22,508,371	$12,127,362	($10,381,009)

Source – United States Census Bureau - U.S. Trade in Goods by Country

Top Trade Surplus Nations – 1992-2012

Country	Imports (millions)	Exports (millions)	Cumulative Surplus/ (Deficit)
Netherlands	$258,140	$515,851	$257,711
Hong Kong	$177,221	$366,757	$189,535
Australia	$137,139	$323,704	$186,566
Belgium	$231,029	$367,792	$136,763
United Arab Emirates	$23,413	$139,207	$115,794
Singapore	$354,119	$414,398	$60,278
Panama	$7,134	$61,159	$54,025
Egypt	$28,960	$82,452	$53,492
Argentina	$66,917	$108,239	$41,321
Turkey	$72,252	$111,781	$39,529
Chile	$98,999	$126,783	$27,784
Brazil	$370,374	$395,988	$25,613
Bahamas	$9,328	$33,177	$23,849
Jamaica	$12,390	$32,864	$20,473
Paraguay	$1,295	$19,738	$18,442
Qatar	$8,210	$23,291	$15,080
Gibraltar	$62	$14,823	$14,761
Greece	$14,070	$28,798	$14,728
Lebanon	$1,463	$16,033	$14,570
Dominican Republic	$82,775	$95,993	$13,218
Afghanistan	$690	$10,115	$9,426
Morocco	$9,772	$19,022	$9,250
Bermuda	$733	$9,830	$9,097
Cayman Islands	$389	$8,862	$8,473
Luxembourg	$7,546	$15,749	$8,203
Total 1992-2012	**$1,974,422**	**$3,342,405**	**$1,367,984**

Source – United States Census Bureau - U.S. Trade in Goods by Country

Other Resources

The following are a few of the resources used in pulling together the information cited in this book...I hope you find them useful.

The U.S. Census Bureau – www.census.gov

The U.S. Bureau of Labor Statistics – www.bls.gov

The Government Accounting Office – www.gao.gov

The Cato Institute – www.cato.org

If you are interested in keeping up with the economic measures presented in this book, please check out the web site. The plan is to keep adding to the resource list and to continue to monitor the data the rest of the world wants to avoid...

www.exportingprosperity.com

About The Author

James H. Boudreau has had a diverse, if not storied, career in marketing, sales and entrepreneurship. He began working in retail selling computers and ultimately moved on to executive level positions in the video game and computer game industries. At age 33 he "left it all behind" to obtain an MBA from Northeastern University. After graduating in 1996 he pursued a career in consulting and entrepreneurship, launching dozens of businesses and thousands of products. He also taught marketing and entrepreneurship for 10 years as a part-time lecturer at Northeastern University.

Beyond his "traditional credentials", the author has devoted countless hours to doing volunteer in the community and working with entrepreneurs to help them realize their dreams. In 2011 he finally began to pursue his passion for writing finishing this book in 2013.